The Project Management Office (PMO) as a pop-up shop

How to become an Agile PMO with fast, flexible and structured value in projects & programmes.

Mertine Middelkoop

Including useful checklists, 11 templates and 15 task overviews.

Editions: 1st edition, May 2013 (Dutch version "Project Management Office als pop-up shop" ISBN: 9789461939364)
August 2014 English translation
To be ordered at: www.pmoportal.nl
ISBN: 9781500144111

Author: Mertine Middelkoop
Publisher and cover design: Mero Management BV
Copyright © 2014 by Mertine Middelkoop

Cover illustration: 123RF.com
Photo author: Denise Keus
Translation by: Maybritt Kiel

No part of this work may be reproduced, transmitted or made public by any person or entity, by any information storage and retrieval system, in any form or by any means, electronic, mechanical, photocopying, recording, scanning or otherwise, without prior written permission of the author.
Whilst every care has been taken when writing this work, errors may be found. The publisher and author disclaim liability for any damages occurred by possible errors and/or inaccuracies in this work.

The tasks of a PMO employee are like the strings of an instrument, not too loose and not too tight.

Inspired by Buddha

WISH

A book is two-way traffic. I hope that this book helps you as a reader to improve yourself in the PMO business or to support others. As an author I have learned a lot whilst writing and I hope to learn even more from comments and suggestions from you the reader. I look forward hearing from you.

mertine.middelkoop@gmail.com
www.pmoportal.nl

Contents

FOREWORD BY SUE VOWLER I

FOREWORD BY PETER TAYLOR III

1. INTRODUCTION 1

2. THE POP-UP PMO 5

3. WHO AND WHAT (TARGET GROUP AND OBJECTIVE) 8

4. FOCUSSING ON PROJECT OBJECTIVE, GOVERNANCE & RESULT GIVES PROJECT SUCCESS 14

5. PMO THROUGH 3D GLASSES AND HOW A PMO EMPLOYEE FITS IN 19

6. A POP-UP PMO IN 10 STEPS 25
    - 6.1 STEP 1: INTAKE(S) BETWEEN THE PMO EMPLOYEE & PROJECT MANAGER 25
    - 6.2 STEP 2: ESTABLISHING PMO OBJECTIVES AND SERVICES (BUILDING BLOCKS) 26
    - 6.3 STEP 3: GATHER INFORMATION AND FURTHER ACQUAINTANCES 27
    - 6.4 STEP 4: SET UP PMO PLAN OF ACTION 27
    - 6.5 STEP 5: CONFIGURE PROJECT PROCESSES (SERVICES) 28
    - 6.6 STEP 6: CONFIGURE THE POP-UP PMO ORGANISATION 29
    - 6.7 STEP 7: CONFIGURE PMO TOOLS & TECHNIQUES 30
    - 6.8 STEP 8: CONFIGURE PMO INFORMATION & COMMUNICATION 30
    - 6.9 STEP 9: VERIFY AND IMPLEMENT PMO PLAN OF ACTION 31
    - 6.10 STEP 10: COMMUNICATE THE TEMPORARY PMO SERVICES 31

7. MANAGING THE POP-UP PMO 33

8. BUILDING BLOCKS: PROJECT PROCESSES (FUNCTIONS & SERVICES) 38
    - 8.1 CLARIFICATION TO THE PARAGRAPHS IN CHAPTER 9 AND 10 42

9. BUILDING BLOCKS: PLANNING 45
    - 9.1 PROJECT SET-UP & CLOSURE 45
    - *EVERYTHING COMES TO AN END SOMETIME* 48
    - 9.2 STAKEHOLDER MANAGEMENT AND COMMUNICATION 51
    - *COMMUNICATION IS THE KEY FACTOR TO GET SUPPORT AND INFORMATION* 53
    - 9.3 PLANNING 57
    - *IF YOU ARE FAILING TO PLAN, THEN YOU ARE PLANNING TO FAIL* 59
    - 9.4 RESOURCE MANAGEMENT 65
    - *NO PROJECT WITHOUT RESOURCES* 67
    - 9.5 BENEFIT MANAGEMENT 73
    - *REPEAT THE "WHY" QUESTION REGULARLY* 76

10. BUILDING BLOCKS: DELIVERY 79
    - 10.1 REPORTING 79
    - *THE RIGHT OF REPORTING* 81
    - 10.2 RISK MANAGEMENT 85
    - *WHEN YOU CAN IDENTIFY A RISK, YOU CAN ALSO MITIGATE IT* 87
    - 10.3 ISSUE MANAGEMENT 91
    - *THE ISSUE MANAGEMENT PROCESS IS A MAJOR ARTERY OF THE PROJECT* 93

	10.4	CHANGE MANAGEMENT 97

ORGANISE THE CHANGE MANAGEMENT PROCESS IN ADVANCE TO AVOID PROJECT FAILURE 99
    10.5   FINANCE 103
IT IS NOT ABOUT HOW MUCH BUDGET YOU HAVE BUT ABOUT WHAT YOU CAN DO WITH IT 105
    10.6   QUALITY ASSURANCE 109
QUALITY IS AS GOOD AS THE WEAKEST LINK 112
    10.7   INFORMATION & CONFIGURATION MANAGEMENT 117
DOES YOUR PROJECT FILE LOOK LIKE THE CUTLERY DRAWER AT HOME? 119
    10.8   TRANSITION MANAGEMENT 125
OPERATION SUCCESSFUL, PATIENT DECEASED 128
    10.9   KNOWLEDGE MANAGEMENT 131
ACQUIRE, MONITOR AND SECURE KNOWLEDGE BEFORE, DURING AND AFTER A PROJECT 134
    10.10   SECRETARIAT 137
WHETHER OR NOT SECRETARIAT ACTIVITIES? 139
A HATE-LOVE AFFAIR WITH THE STEERING COMMITTEE 140

11.   ALONG WITH EVERYONE: THE ORGANISING OF A WORKSHOP 143

    11.1   PROJECT KICK-OFF WITH STEERING COMMITTEE MEMBERS 148
    11.2   TEMPLATE: WORKSHOP INTAKE FORM 151

12.   SIZE MATTERS. HOW MANY ARE NEEDED FOR THE PMO? 153

13.   PMO EMPLOYEE COMPETENCES & PERSONAL GOALS 156

    13.1   PERSONAL LEARNING GOALS 164
    13.2   PROFILING HELPS YOU ACHIEVE YOUR GOALS 167
    13.3   SEVEN TIPS FOR PERSONAL PROFILING 169

14.   PROJECT MANAGER AND PMO EMPLOYEE; THE GOLDEN DUO 171

    14.1   CAPTAINITIS 173
    14.2   THE FEAR TO DELEGATE 175

15.   FOUR TIMES PASSION FOR PMO 177

OVERVIEW TEMPLATES AND CHECKLISTS 180

APPENDIX A: GLOSSARY 181

APPENDIX B: INTAKE FORM BETWEEN PROJECT MANAGER & PMO EMPLOYEE 186

APPENDIX C: TEMPLATE POP-UP PMO OBJECTIVES AND AGREEMENTS 196

APPENDIX D: POP-UP PMO SETUP CHECKLIST 197

APPENDIX E: POP-UP PMO CLOSURE CHECKLIST 202

SOURCES 205

ACKNOWLEDGEMENTS 208

INDEX 209

FOREWORD by Sue Vowler

Writing P3O and seeing it published by the Office of Government Commerce (now Axelos) was the culmination of several years lobbying that PMOs are run by professional people and working in a PMO or Portfolio Office is a career path in its own right.

P3O was enthusiastically received by the PMO community, many of whom said I had given them a voice or a belief in their expertise and value to organisations. So it is great to see other publications both supporting and building on the principles that P3O laid down.

Temporary **programme or project offices** are set up to support a new initiative and may be a team for a large programme or a single person supporting a programme or project manager. They only exist for the life of the delivery of the programme or project and they may be staffed from a central flexible resource pool or use locally sourced people who follow standards set by the Centre of Excellence.

The "Project Management Office as a pop up shop" is a great analogy and perfectly describes the world of the temporary programme or project office. It fills the gaps in P3O, answering the "how do I do this?" question, and is a true practitioners guide to setting up, running and closing down temporary PMOs.

It is not an academic tome, it is a real practitioners book, full of really useful checklists and working practices and expressed in a way that will appeal to practitioners in the throes of setting up and running their first or subsequent PMO. I particularly commend chapters 8, 9 and 10 which take PMO services and functions and turn them into reality with action plans, processes, tools and techniques. This book is a very practical contribution to the world of PMOs to be read and dipped into on a daily basis.

Sue Vowler

Author Portfolio Programme and Project Offices (P3O)
Director Project Angels Limited

www.project-angels.co.uk and www.p3o-officialsite.com

FOREWORD by Peter Taylor

As the author of Leading Successful PMOs (Gower) and the creator/leader of 3 major PMOs over the last few years I have seen the value of the PMO rising to the front of organisations attention in the delivery of strategic initiatives through project based activity. And this is a good thing; I really believe that it is.

But there remains a lot of misunderstanding about what a PMO can be and even more about how a PMO can be created and tuned for each organisation and each project. Right now the demand for PMO expertise outstrips the proven experience that is in the marketplace, and this is a risk to the continued value representation of PMOs in businesses around the world.

'The Project Management Office (PMO) as a pop-up shop' by Mertine Middelkoop aids in this situation by providing readers with one possible scenario to get to their own pop-up PMO up and running fast, through a simple to follow, and easy to understand, PMO roadmap.

One of the types of PMOs that I speak of in my own book is that of the 'Special Purpose' PMO and now that I have read Mertine's book I will start talking about 'Pop-Up PMOs' because this is a great analogy, seeing modern pop-up shops in the same light as temporary PMOs.

The book provides many practical examples as well as tools and templates that readers can use at their will as they follow along the roadmap to PMO success. And wish all of you who build and lead or support such PMOs all the best possible luck, it is a tough but rewarding job and a very important one. Just add to that luck with some wise advice such as this book: The Project Management Office (PMO) as a pop-up shop.

Peter 'The Lazy Project Manager' Taylor

www.leadingsuccessfulpmos.com and www.peterbtaylor.co.uk

1. INTRODUCTION

Everyone wants happiness, no one wants pain,
but you can't make a rainbow without a little rain.
Zion Lee

I remember it as clearly as if it had happened yesterday, my first few weeks as a Project Management Office (PMO) employee on a project. There they called it project management officer as it sounded more important and, because I was seconded, they could consequently ask a higher rate for me. The project objective was to merge five government agencies, including their applications and systems, into one central unit. A big project of one and a half years full of organisational, technical and facility challenges. Being overly ambitious, I started the task, thinking: I can easily do this, as, after all, I have a lot of experience as a consultant, communications officer and a project manager. Therefore, being a project management officer should work, right?

In hindsight I have to conclude that during my first project as a project management officer, or rather a PMO employee, I had forgotten to do and manage quite a bit. There was no change management process, there were no agreements on document naming, virtually no thoughts on project communication, nor on many other matters. I thought: this is the job of a project manager; he or she will do it.
Up to 2010 there were hardly any books written or training provided for PMO employees. In each and every new project following, I continued learning through trial and error. Whether it was about a massive move, an organisational change, building something specific or developing software, every time the same sort of processes have to be put in place and implemented. I also noticed enormous differences between project managers in what they did themselves, what they did not think of and what they asked me, the PMO employee, to do.

PMO turns out to be a specific business capability on its own and luckily more and more organisations and trainers agree. It is a capability that at times is still wrongly undervalued at which project managers look disrespectfully. It is sometimes seen as a step up to project management.
I will continue using the name PMO employee throughout this book for this specific role within a project or programme.

In a later stage of my career I did notice certain matters in regards to project control of the project manager who in my opinion could do better, but I did not always have the courage to say anything to the, at times, authoritarian project manager. I thought to be mistaken and was clearly no sparring partner yet to the project manager of that time.

Both should complement, communicate and believe in each other and trust that the other will deliver what is expected.

1. INTRODUCTION

The PMO employee can be the project manager's coach and vice versa. Both are capable in the field of project management, with each their own special competences that make the project succeed. This equality in functions is being supported by the publication of "Competence profiles, Certification levels and Functions in the Project Management and Project Support Field – Based on ICB version 3 – 2nd edition" by IPMA in 2011 and by the in 2008 published Axelos best practice "Portfolio, Programme and Project Offices: P3O®".
IPMA is an association with members who work together to further develop their own professionalism and the field of project, programme and portfolio management. Axelos (the formerly OGC: Office of Government Commerce) has also marketed, besides P3O, a number of Best Practices like ITIL®, PRINCE2®, MoP® and MSP®.
The term PMO is an all-purpose word and has many perceptions.

In the IPMA Competence profile book several different types of PMO organisational forms are being distinguished. These terms are also used in P3O:
1. Portfolio office with various kinds of functions:
    - A. Central office focused on strategic support and knowledge centre.
    - B. Temporary PMOs to launch new initiatives.
    - C. Central portfolio office with satellite offices (for big organisations and with more permanent decentralised offices).
2. Temporary project or programme office or employees in a supporting role.
3. Virtual PMO with support from individual employees coming from different functional departments. PMO is not a separate department.
4. Single office (office with one or few people, usually aimed at offering training or the application of project methodologies).

These types of PMOs can be applied to a:
- **Project:** a temporary organisation that has been set up to provide a pre-defined result within the conditions specified.
- **Programme:** a temporary organisation that has been set up for the coordination, control and monitoring of the implementation of a coherent number of projects and activities in order to achieve results and benefits that add to the strategic objectives of the organisation.
- **Multiproject:** is comprised of a number of incoherent projects of which the resources are to be managed effectively.
- **Portfolio:** a set of existing and future projects and programmes to maximise the objectives of the organisation with the resources available.

In the IPMA Competence profile book and in P3O several PMO roles are described, I will discuss these in further detail in chapter 13 "PMO competences & personal goals".

N.B.: the book you are reading now is about option 2 (temporary project or programme office or employees in a supporting role at a project or programme, whether or not virtual). This temporary project or programme office can be delivered from a permanent central PMO. Provided that such a permanent PMO is present and the delivery of temporary support to projects and programmes is part of its service catalogue.

1. INTRODUCTION

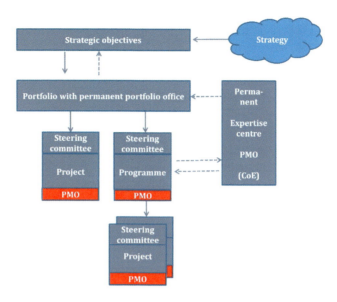

Figure 1.1 Types of PMOs being discussed in this book (in red)

Some other terms are:
- Decentralised PMO
- Temporary PMO
- An external PMO
- Project Support Office (PSO)
- Special purpose PMO
- Pop-up PMO

At present my bookcase is filled with a whole range of books about projects, programmes and portfolio offices. Especially books on setting up permanent PMOs at an organisational and tactical level. However, I missed a practical guide that particularly zooms in on the operational aspects of temporary, continuously recurring situations that come with a project.

I compare every project to setting up a new company in a short period of time. A kind of shop with all its bells and whistles like personnel, logistics, facilities management, communication, planning, suppliers etc. So much needs to be organised.
Nowadays, many different methodologies are available for managing projects and programmes, like:
- Project Management Body of Knowledge (PMBOK guide),
- Projects IN Controlled Environment (PRINCE2),
- Project Driven Creation / "Projectmatig Creëren" (PMC),
- Managing Successful Programmes (MSP),
- Agile (Scrum).

1. INTRODUCTION

For more information see the Dutch book "Wegwijzer voor methoden bij projectmanagement" (Project management methodologies roadmap) by Van Haren Publishing.

These methodologies sometimes only briefly describe the tasks of what a PMO employee could do. As far as they have been mentioned, I have incorporated them in this book.

PRINCE2 only describes a few brief activities with the term "project support", often abbreviated to PSO. These activities are limited to, with all due respect, administrative support, configuration management, updating the schedule, establishing and maintaining records and being an expert in tools and techniques. A fully-fledged PMO role goes far beyond that. PRINCE2 merely describes the "WHAT" whereas the project also needs the "HOW" during the implementation stage and that is what the PMO employee can organise.

In PMBOK they refer to a project office, however, the to-be-supplied support services are not mentioned any further. It only describes the "WHAT".

With Scrum the competencies of a Scrum Master resemble those of a PMO employee.

Although from Axelos (a joint venture company set up by the Cabinet Office and Capita) in PRINCE2 and MSP the work package of a temporary PMO is being discussed, it does not reach far enough to get a quick insight on how to set up a temporary PMO within a project or programme. In P3O a "temporary P3O lifecycle" is being described. Next to this, there are several chapters on tools and techniques, also intended for the temporary P3O.

> No project management method describes the full extent of the possible work package of a PMO employee and how to set up a temporary PMO in a quick and structured manner.

Setting up a PMO position or role is a project within a project. With identification, defining and implementation phases and lead time ranging from a few weeks up to 1-2 months.

This book aims to, whilst looking through a pair of functions and services glasses independently of any method, set up and manage a temporary PMO as well from the perspective of a project manager as from a PMO employee.

> *Not everything you read in this book will be relevant to you.*
> *This book has been intentionally set up broadly for a wide audience, for all possible situations and organisations.*
> *Think of it as a kind of menu from which you can choose.*

2. THE POP-UP PMO

A pop-up shop is a temporary shop that suddenly appears somewhere, adds value to a few stakeholders and eventually disappears again when certain deliverables have been met.

A pop-up shop has a specific objective, just like a project. That can be selling and simply making a profit. Or it can also be increasing brand awareness or raising awareness for a specific subject like sustainability.

In 2011 the store chain Hennes and Mauritz wanted to raise awareness for the basic needs of clean water and proper sanitation in order to show their sustainable entrepreneurship. 25% of the proceeds of their beach collection are given to WaterAid.

The pop-up shops with the best results have established a sound business approach.
- There is a roadmap and material ready.
- Beforehand an analysis is conducted on potential customers, landlord, regulators etc. (stakeholders).
- The objective is clear and known to everyone.
- The assembly of the project team is well thought out per pop-up idea and location.

2. THE POP-UP PMO

A project and the temporary PMO within such a project are, just like a pop-up shop, a temporary organisation at sometimes variable locations. A lot has to be arranged within a short period of time, like:
- Resourcing: accommodation, approvals, personnel.
- Finances: costs, assets, money flows, cash register systems.
- Planning: from when to when is it time to get the shop ready and how long will it stay open?
- Stakeholder management and communication: who are involved (retailer association, landlord, local authority, potential customers, press) and how and when are we advertising?
- Information and configuration management: how do we organise our inventory and how do we price (uniform price tags)?

For a project to be successful, certain basic matters need to be addressed. That is where a temporary PMO can fulfil a role and can realise project control processes and implement tools.

> Just like with pop-up shops and permanent stores, there are similarities between a temporary and permanent PMO. The difference is particularly in the temporary character, the mostly very short setup time, variable locations and alternating cast of project management, team and support. These differences appear to be rather limited at first sight, however, ingredients such as planning, communication and organisation are being thrown in a kind of pressure cooker and moulded into working processes and agreements. The time factor, which is limited, makes setting up a pop-up PMO rather an interesting challenge.

Certain differences between a pop-up PMO and a permanent PMO are:

Temporary PMO	Permanent PMO
Pop-up shop metaphor	Permanent store metaphor
Search a location	Permanent location
Select processes and templates	Established processes and templates
Short initial time (x days) to set up	Longer period to set up (x months)
Varying PMO team	Established PMO team
Scope is one or more projects or a programme	Scope is all or part of established projects portfolio and organisation governance
Select tooling	Established set of tools
Find out who the involved PMO stakeholders are	Involved PMO stakeholders are known
Uses a roadmap	Provides the roadmap to projects
Success is: PMO can schedule to discontinue	Success is: PMO continues

2. THE POP-UP PMO

A project manager can do everything himself or he can outsource it and hire one or more specialists. That specialist is a PMO employee who is at home with many of the processes or it can be a resource with specialist expertise (a planner or project controller).
A resource or group of resources represent the temporary project office or temporary PMO.

The PMO employee, whose job it is to assist the project manager in setting up and managing project control, preferably has a roadmap of the concerning organisation close at hand. This roadmap, with framework, templates, tooling and processes can be delivered by a permanent PMO. All stakeholders and project control processes are mapped beforehand and communication is tuned. And the objective is clear to all stakeholders.

Is that the case? Do you recognise this? Is all set beforehand, is the project design script ready? Do you as a PMO employee know exactly what to do? Does coordinating the activities with the project manager run smoothly? Is your career path clear?
If so, you can now lay down the book and you do not need to continue reading.
For all others I hope that after having read this book you can quickly set up and manage a pop-up PMO in any location, any environment, with any organisation and with any given team members and project manager. And that the PMO profession offers you a very interesting career perspective.

> In this book I mean by a pop-up PMO "The part within a temporary business that takes care of support, expertise and securing project management processes". In other words "a pop-up PMO".
> The involved PMO officials and specialists are "PMO employees".

3. WHO AND WHAT (TARGET GROUP AND OBJECTIVE)

For whom?
This book is for all involved in temporary (project or programme) support. The support can be delivered from a department (permanent PMO) which allocates project resources (or parts of their tasks) to projects. Organisations without a permanent PMO with a pool of resources, hire them elsewhere.

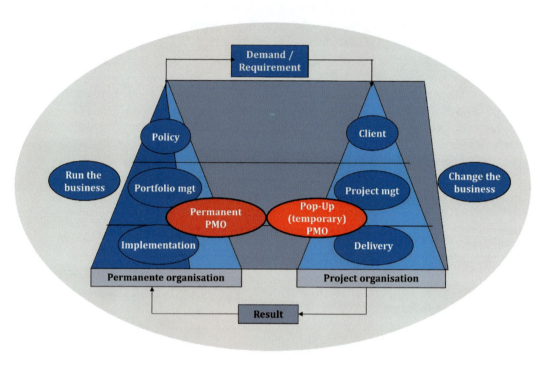

Figure 3.1 Permanent line organisation versus project organisation

Besides PMO employees and heads of PMO, this book is also intended for project and programme managers who need an efficiently set up project office within their project or programme.

What can you ask your PMO (employee) as a project or programme manager? How do you choose and shape the temporary PMO that fits you, your project/programme and the organisation? How can you make more out of your temporary pop-up PMO?

3. WHO AND WHAT (TARGET GROUP AND OBJECTIVE)

Looking at the IPMA competence profiles, in this book I will particularly focus on the following by IPMA mentioned functions that can be found in a pop-up PMO:
- PMO assistant (IPMA level E),
- PMO employee (IPMA level D),
- Senior PMO employee and PM specialist (IPMA level C),
- Head Project or Programme office (IPMA level C and B),
- PM consultant (IPMA level B).

I will summarise them under the header "PMO employee". They will be discussed in further detail in chapter 13 "PMO competences & personal goals".

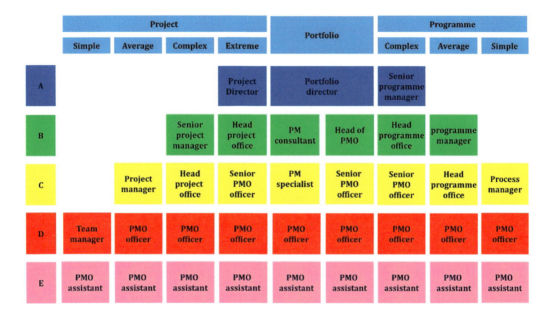

Figure 3.2 IPMA "Competence profiles, Certification levels and Functions in the Project Management and Project Support Field - Based on NCB version 3"

Based on what?

The book is based on the aforementioned IPMA competence profiles, on the P3O methodology, on a matrix of the IPMA NL PMO Special Interest Group Central Netherlands and on my own experience.

P3O is a methodology from Axelos (formerly known as OGC), aligned to the earlier developed methods PRINCE2, Managing Successful Programmes (MSP) and Management of Portfolio (MoP). It can provide practical guidance to especially setting up and designing a permanent PMO.

3. WHO AND WHAT (TARGET GROUP AND OBJECTIVE)

P3O has a chapter about the "temporary P3O lifecycle". Next to this, there are several chapters on tools and techniques, also intended for the temporary P3O. The first official version of the P3O model was published by the OGC in 2008. A new edition has been released in 2013 by Axelos.

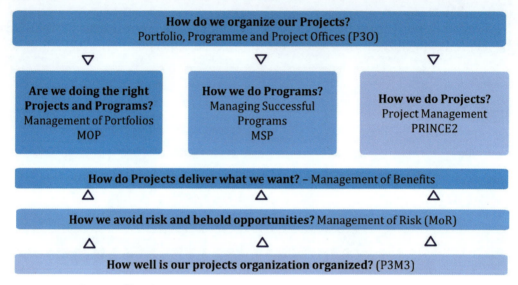

Figure 3.3 Cabinet Office best practices

P3O mentions that when setting up a project or programme, it is best to ask consultancy for the establishment of processes, report cycles, developing plans, facilities and team setup.
P3O clearly distinguishes between a temporary (pop-up) and a permanent PMO. With a pop-up PMO the requirements are different and the PMO needs to fit the size, complexity and criteria of the project or programme concerned.

The temporary PMO knows several stakeholders. When I interpret the manual, I get to the following pop-up PMO stakeholder model:

3. WHO AND WHAT (TARGET GROUP AND OBJECTIVE)

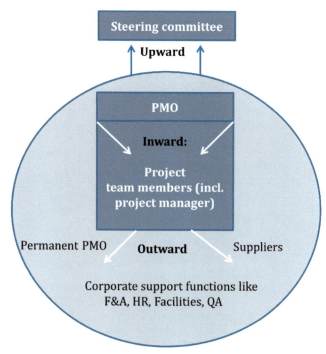

Figure 3.4 Stakeholders at a pop-up PMO conform P3O

In the P3O manual, appendix F "Functions and Services" describes the processes that can take place in a project, programme or portfolio. The relevant processes for a project or programme form the foundation of the building blocks that are being further discussed in chapter 8 "Building blocks: Project processes (functions & services)".

Complementary to the IPMA book "Competence profiles, Certification levels and Functions in the Project Management and Project Support Field - based on ICB version 3", the IPMA NL PMO Special Interest Group Central Netherlands has designed a matrix[1] of task areas and possible responsibilities for Project Management Officers. This is actually a matrix for 3 types of PMO employees (portfolio, programme and project) and for 3 different levels (junior, mid and senior). The matrix for programme and project support officer has been consulted for all levels when writing this book.

---

[1] The matrix is free to download from www.PMwiki.nl.

3. WHO AND WHAT (TARGET GROUP AND OBJECTIVE)

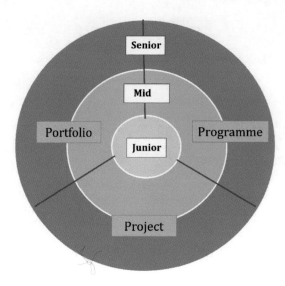

Figure 3.5 "PMO profiles matrix" source: IPMA NL PMO Special Interest Group Central Netherlands

When you zoom in on the tasks for programme and project PMO, you get the following figure.

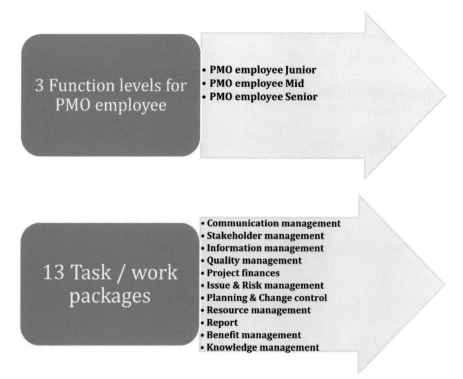

Figure 3.6 "PMO function and task matrix" source: IPMA NL PMO Special Interest Group Central Netherlands for the 3 function levels

3. WHO AND WHAT (TARGET GROUP AND OBJECTIVE)

How can this book help you?
This book is useful for all types of projects and programmes, for example:
- Fixed price projects.
- With a high risk.
- Infrastructure projects.
- Technical migrations.
- Facility projects.
- Organisation changes.
- For software developing projects.
- When you need to conform to the governance of a company, however you do not know how.

> Goal of a PMO:
> The right information at the right time in the right hands.
> James Brown

By structurally setting up a pop-up PMO you will get the project off to a flying start. Within a short time (from 2 weeks up to 2 months) the control of the project will be clear and communicable to all team members and other stakeholders. And unambiguously presentable for a project kick-off.

> The PMO "**CREATE**"
>
> **C**ontrol of project progress
> Lowers **R**isks
> Gives **E**nergy
> Realises **A**ccuracy
> Brings **T**ransparency
> Establishes **G**overnance and Compliance

N.B. For readability purposes, this book will simply be about projects, unless it specifically relates to a programme.

4. FOCUSSING ON PROJECT OBJECTIVE, GOVERNANCE & RESULT GIVES PROJECT SUCCESS

For project success, three questions are crucial:
1. **Why:** Organisations that communicate about the why turn out to be more successful than organisations that do not do this, according to the researcher Simon Sinek. Therefore, always set the why-question at the centre, why do we undertake this project? In other words "the project objective".
2. **How:** A fitting, aligned and for all involved known project control. How do we do this project? I.e. "the project governance".
3. **What**: Focus on the end product. What will be delivered at the end of the project? In other words "the project result".

When these three matters are secured, any obstacle during the project can easier be overcome and the project can successfully be closed/realised.

As a PMO employee you will contribute to getting these three crucial matters clear.

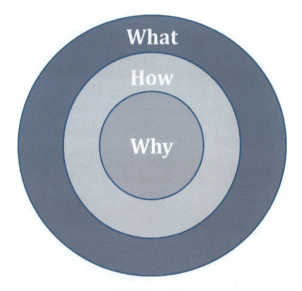

Figure 4.1 Start with why, by Simon Sinek

The objective of the project result should be known to all involved. Projects rather have (in the issue of the day) the tendency to be turned inwards and directed on activities. Benefit management, stakeholder management, quality management, kick-off workshops, the business case and a well-functioning steering committee are tools that help keeping an eye on the final result (desired outcome) of a project.

With every crisis, confrontation, deviation, issue, risk or decision to be taken during the project, can be returned to "Why do we do this project?".
The second aspect of importance is the "business governance". Every organisation has a "Corporate governance".

4. FOCUSSING ON PROJECT OBJECTIVE, GOVERNANCE & RESULT GIVES PROJECT SUCCESS

> Corporate governance involves a set of relationships between a company's management, its board, its shareholders and other stakeholders. Corporate governance also provides the structure through which the objectives of the company are set, and the means of attaining those objectives and monitoring performance are determined.
>
> *From: Project Governance, Ralf Müller, Gower Publishing, 2009.*

We read here that at corporate level it is about stakeholders and structure in order to monitor and realise organisation objectives (strategy).
The governance of project management is a subset of activities that are involved in the total corporate governance (of the entire company).

What does professional literature say about project governance?

> The governance of project management concerns those areas of corporate governance that are specifically related to project activities. Effective governance of project management ensures that an organisation's project portfolio is aligned to the organisation's objectives, is delivered efficiently and is sustainable. Governance of project management also supports the means by which the board, and other major project stakeholders, are provided with timely, relevant and reliable information.
>
> *From: Directing Change, A guide to Governance of Project Management, by the Association for Project Management (APM), 2005*

This definition presumes the perspective of a corporate board. It offers, in a mature project organisation, a certain project control structure and needs information in order to align and keep the project portfolio aligned with the strategic organisation objectives.

From the perspective of the project itself, the following provides a close definition of project governance.

4. FOCUSSING ON PROJECT OBJECTIVE, GOVERNANCE & RESULT GIVES PROJECT SUCCESS

> Project governance is the framework within which project decisions are made.
>
> *Project Governance: A Practical Guide to Effective Project Decision Making by Ross Garland, Kogan Page, London, Philadelphia, 2009*

In workshops and training I prefer to explain it as follows:

> Project governance includes the structures, roles and responsibilities in order to be able to take decisions in a project.

Without a well-set up project governance, projects are doomed to fail from the onset. The project manager needs to enforce that this is well regulated. The PMO employee can give advice and be of support here. The PMO can help to successfully realise projects. A project management method can help with this aspect to a large extent. However, the project governance goes a step further whereby a methodology is merely a part of the entire organisation around projects. What functions, roles, responsibilities, capabilities, consultation bodies etc. are there to support the methodology?

Sometimes you also see that the project governance is set up, however nobody keeps to it. So-called PINO projects (Prince In Name Only) are a well-known example of this. This is characteristic of projects and organisations with a low maturity level in the field of project control.

In figure 4.2 I have summarised how these different governances are in proportion to each other.

4. FOCUSSING ON PROJECT OBJECTIVE, GOVERNANCE & RESULT GIVES PROJECT SUCCESS

Figure 4.2 Coherent corporate and project governance

Questions to be addressed and answered at the start of a project are:
- Who has final responsibility (accountable) for the project success?
- How is the decision-making set up? How is the accountability set up?
- Who has got which role? Client, supplier, end user(s), project manager, stakeholders, project controller?
- What escalation and consultation structures are there?
- How are the project management tools being used? Monitoring and reporting about main products, the most important milestones, necessary reviews and both financial and content approval.
- Who reports to whom, at what moment?
- What are the process agreements on issues, errors, changes, risks, financial matters and resource management?

For a well-functioning pop-up PMO and of course also project, it is of importance that this is clear. The PMO employee can use the questionnaire in appendix B "Intake form between project manager and PMO employee". In case the project manager cannot answer these, the questions can be raised as an item on the agenda in the steering committee or raised by the project manager during a meeting with the client.
Another method that I have positive experiences with is to raise these questions during a workshop with management of the contracting company or business part. Of course, if possible, before the project starts. Such a workshop can also be with the members of the steering committee, preferably in a wider assembly with the steering committee's management.

4. FOCUSSING ON PROJECT OBJECTIVE, GOVERNANCE & RESULT GIVES PROJECT SUCCESS

You can facilitate this workshop in the role of a PMO employee.

> **Creating a sound governance structure
> before the start of a project is of vital importance
> to the success of a project.**

*In my early years as a PMO employee I was sometimes only employed when the project was already at full steam and the project manager was too busy.
Often the governance was defined in the project initiation document (PID), however, that was where it stopped. The project governance was insufficiently optimised and secured within the line and project organisation.*

*Nowadays, before the start of a project, I meet up with project leaders, members of the steering committee and clients in order to define the project governance on the basis of the P3O® services and functions.
Everyone knows now, even before there is a single letter of the project plan written on paper, the ins and outs in order to run the project efficiently.*

5. PMO THROUGH 3D GLASSES AND HOW A PMO EMPLOYEE FITS IN

Rightly or wrongly, the acronym PMO is being used for all sorts of work and departments. Everyone has their own perception of what this could mean. These perceptions can sometimes be very far apart from each other. Some of the names around the term PMO employee that I have encountered over the years are:
- Project manager supporter (or officer)
- Project supporter
- Manager project management
- Project secretary
- Project / Programme support officer
- Project / Programme supporter
- Project office employee
- Portfolio (management) officer
- Project controller
- Project assurance officer
- Planner
- Specialised names like planner, project controller, risk manager
- Project assistant (PA)
- PSO-employee

In terms of content of the work, experience and competences required, the differences between the functions can be great. Without judging, anyone can imagine that working on a portfolio of projects is different than working on a project itself.

Looking at the work of a PMO employee, 3 dimensions become apparent.
1. Organisation: Where in the organisation is the work carried out and how mature is the project organisation?
2. Task: What kinds of tasks are being carried out?
3. People: What is the level (level of difficulty) of the PMO activities?

5. PMO THROUGH 3D GLASSES AND HOW A PMO EMPLOYEE FITS IN

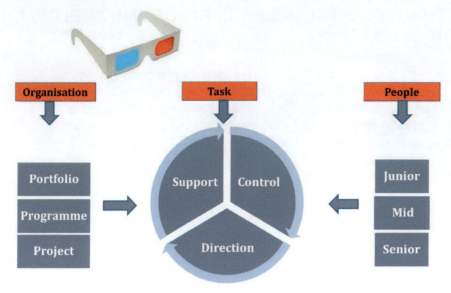

Figure 5.1 The PMO field of expertise is 3-dimensional: Organisation, Task and People level

1. Organisation
You should wonder at what level in the organisation the tasks take place, whether or not from a permanent PMO. Is this in or for the benefit of:
a. Project
b. Programme
c. Portfolio
Or perhaps a combination?

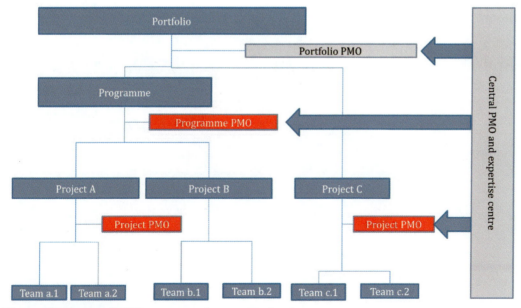

Figure 5.2 Types of PMOs as regards to organisation

5. PMO THROUGH 3D GLASSES AND HOW A PMO EMPLOYEE FITS IN

It can occur in organisations that a pop-up PMO, under the direction of a permanent PMO, is being made available to projects and programmes. As if it were pop-up shops under direction of a holding. The permanent PMO provides project guidelines, is the central source of information and can co-monitor the quality of the project implementation.

Where there is no central PMO, the projects and programme PMOs develop themselves as independent shops, without support or direction. At the very most, the organisation governance will give some direction.

When the project or programme is ready, the Pop-up PMO will cease to exist (just like the project, programme itself).

Another aspect at organisation level is the degree of maturity of the project organisation. There are several models and methodologies to determine these, like CMMI and P3M3, which usually come down to 5 different levels.

Degree of maturity[2]	Characteristics
1. Ad hoc	No processes, no templates, no standards, no monitoring. The project manager sets up the project on one's own discretion. No project management governance present in the organisation.
2. Repeatable	Basic processes and procedures. Reactive way of delivering support. Basic reports.
3. Defined and controllable	Standard way of project management implementation. Proactive support is being provided to projects. Mostly permanent PMO present. Process improvement is taking place based on a qualitative analysis.
4. Controlled	Integration between projects and operation, i.e. between change and Business as Usual (BAU). Permanent PMO (or other quality controller) present. The process is being systematically measured in order to ascertain and improve deviations. Process improvement is taking place based on a quantitative analysis.
5. Optimising	Systematic process improvement based on measurements has become an integrated part of management. New technologies can be introduced in a controlled way. A permanent PMO gives direction and has vision on the project management field of expertise.

---

[2] Leading successful PMOs, Peter Taylor

5. PMO THROUGH 3D GLASSES AND HOW A PMO EMPLOYEE FITS IN

Depending on the degree of maturity of the organisation, you will, as a pop-up PMO, have to do more or less extra work yourself. A mature organisation has a standard project management methodology. There are guidelines "that is how we do a project within our organisation". And there are usable procedures and templates. If there is a permanent PMO present, you can request for them or you will have them delivered. That will then save you a lot of work and you do not have to invent the wheel all over again. Also with all kinds of other questions or requests for extra PMO employees (after approval by a project manager) you can possibly go to such a permanent PMO. You can then set up your pop-up PMO more rapidly.

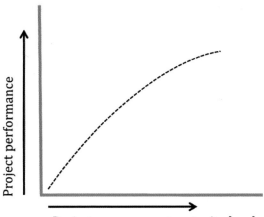

In several publications[3], it can be read that the more mature an organisation is, the bigger the chance of successful projects and also the easier it is to set up the temporary PMO. Several institutes amongst which Gartner, declare that project organisations can only mature with a permanent PMO.
With reorganisations and introducing new methods and technologies, an organisation almost always falls back one or more levels (unless they are at level 5).

2. Task:
There are 3 types of tasks[4] for a PMO employee, which you see reflected in all sorts of PMOs that perform such tasks. It is possible that a PMO progresses over time through these task groups or employs a blended mix.

---

[3] Researching the Value of Project Management, PMI, Mullaly and Thomas, 2009
Portfolio, Programme and Project Management Maturity Model – P3M3, Rod Sowden, Axelos, 2013
Project Management Survey Report, KPMG, July 2013
[4] Leading successful PMOs, Peter Taylor

5. PMO THROUGH 3D GLASSES AND HOW A PMO EMPLOYEE FITS IN

a. Support giving. Provides support in the form of "expertise on demand", like templates, best practices, access to information and expertise from other projects. This works in organisations where projects are successful and where extra control is not deemed necessary. Terms like "Centre of knowledge" and "Project counter" fit here.

b. Controlling. This contains strong quality assurance aspects. An opinion is being formed about activities, processes, procedures, documentation etc. and, where necessary, improved. A PMO provides support and demands that this support is being used. Necessary then is the use of a specific method, templates, forms, conformity to the governance (management agreements) and application of other rules from the PMO. From a permanent PMO regular reviews can be done within the projects. The controlling tasks can only be successfully carried out when:
    1. It is clear in the organisation that the enforcement of the rules will improve the projects and the organisation as a whole.
    2. The PMO has sufficient senior management support that fully supports the tasks.

With a pop-up PMO you see the controlling tasks reflected in configuration and information management, quality management and monitoring of registers.

c. Guiding and steering. Goes even further than control and "takes over" the project by providing project management experience and resources to manage the project. An organisation is committed to itself to appoint professional project managers from a permanent PMO to projects. This gives an enormous input to professionalising the projects because every project manager comes from and reports to the same permanent PMO. In practice it guarantees a high level of consistency across all projects. This is effective in bigger organisations that often know a diversity of support in different areas. And where it fits into the culture. This type of permanent PMOs is especially apparent in America.

With a pop-up PMO a senior PMO employee can temporarily be hired in order to set up the PMO. You could regard the setup work as guiding and steering.

3. People:
How mature is the specific PMO employee in implementing the tasks?

a. Junior PMO employees look after the shop (put very bluntly). This under guidance of the project manager or more senior PMO employee. This can be a tough job depending on the sort of shop! It is not possible for a junior to replace a programme management officer.

b. Mid PMO employees are capable to proactively roll out the needed governance in the project in consultation with the project or programme managers. They are a sparring partner to project and programme managers. And come with improvement initiatives within the environment in which they sit.

5. PMO THROUGH 3D GLASSES AND HOW A PMO EMPLOYEE FITS IN

c. Senior PMO employees look further than the environment in which they sit. They can operate multiple, bigger, more complex projects and programmes. They come, certainly from permanent PMOs, with proposals to improve the governance and quality of the projects in the organisation. They are therefore a sparring partner at management and director level.

With a pop-up PMO, the PMO employee's first responsibility lies of course with their own project or programme. Depending on the complexity of the project or programme, a junior, mid or senior PMO employee will be recruited. Basically you as a PMO employee do not interfere with the BAU/line organisation. You can take note of improvements and possibly also identify and assist, however, interfering with the line organisation is not your job! Unless you have been enlisted for this purpose by your client (and the project should produce this result).

6. A POP-UP PMO IN 10 STEPS

It is only the first step that is difficult.
Marie De Vichy-Chaconne

> An organisation has a great idea to set up a pop-up shop and has hired a project manager for this purpose. In order to start, the project manager adds a PMO employee (project supporter) to his team.
> The project supporter has done this before and gets out the roadmap of the pop-up shop.

A pop-up PMO can be implemented in 10 steps. These 10 steps provide a sequence; however, with most implementations these steps run criss-crossed through each other after the intake (step 1). Nevertheless, you always go through them.

Phase	Step	Action
Identification	1	Intake(s) with the project manager
	2	Establish the temporary PMO objectives and services as agreed with the project manager (building blocks)
	3	Gather information and further acquaintances
Defining	4	Set up PMO plan of action (extension step 2)
	5	Configure project processes (services)
	6	Configure pop-up PMO organisation
	7	Configure required PMO tools & techniques
	8	Configure required PMO information & communication
Implementation	9	Verify and implement PMO plan
	10	Communicate the temporary PMO services
Managing the pop-up PMO (chapter 7)		

6.1 Step 1: Intake(s) between the PMO employee & project manager

The intake is a crucial step in which the mutual expectations are being created. You should ensure that as a starting PMO employee you get the control and global content of the project clear, as quickly as possible. In this step you make agreements with the programme or project manager, who does what (division of tasks: what will the project manager do, what will the PMO employee do).

6. A POP-UP PMO IN 10 STEPS

You can ask questions about four areas:
1. General questions about the project and the organisational environment to get a good picture. What partnerships are there.
2. General PMO expectations, control and budget.
3. Tooling and facilities.
4. Assess and ask for coordination per project process. Who does what, when and how.

To give an idea of the sort of questions you could ask, you can consult the aforementioned appendix B "Intake form between project manager and PMO employee".

A project manager cannot always divide his attention as evenly across the different tasks. For example, in a certain period planning will require more attention than elaborating documents which will then be published (too) late because of this. Depending on the workload or need of the project manager, certain tasks will be outsourced to the PMO employee(s). Additionally, there are tasks that are not always easy to assign by the project manager (writing a plan of action, cost-benefit analysis). Also the available expertise of a PMO employee will determine then to what extent a project manager assigns tasks. More about expertise & division of tasks in chapter 14 "Project manager and PMO employee: the golden duo".

6.2 Step 2: Establishing PMO objectives and services (building blocks)

During the discussion with the project manager expectations have been expressed and agreements have been made. Which services will the temporary PMO implement for the project? As a starting point you can use the possible building blocks (services) from chapter 8 "Building blocks: Project processes (functions & services)". Which tasks will the project manager do him or herself? Are there tasks assigned in the BAU organisation that the PMO does not need to do? If there are tasks assigned to BAU, they can then be classified as PMO tasks and the concerning employees are thence implementing PMO tasks, in other words: they are PMO employees and are supposed to bill the hours to the project. However, this is often not recognised as such nor set up. I often do notice that it is wise as PMO to keep the control over these tasks.

To what extent should the PMO:
- Give support?
- Control?
- Give direction and advice or guidance?

You can actually use a work package description for this or the template from appendix C "Pop-up PMO objectives and agreements".

6. A POP-UP PMO IN 10 STEPS

6.3 Step 3: Gather information and further acquaintances

If all has gone well, you now know more about the project and the organisation behind it. You can now meet and acquaint with other people and departments involved, gather information and make complementary agreements.

You can think in particular of financial departments, or controllers, quality managers, recruitment, facility management etc. This is very important to do, so you will not be taken by surprise later on due to matters having to be done differently than expected.

The aim is to gather as much information on existing processes to which the project must connect. And possibly make process agreements on connecting the project with the relevant existing organisational processes.

6.4 Step 4: Set up PMO plan of action

It is now clear which processes and services the PMO is going to deliver and how you can, or even have to, connect with the line organisation.

You can also, based on the answers from the initial discussion, determine how many hours are needed to set up the PMO and you can make a first estimation of how many hours are thereafter needed to keep the PMO operating. This has possibly already been budgeted at the start of the project or in the tender. It is good to keep this as a starting point for the boundaries of your plan of action and also to manage, based on this, expectations.

> How much time is needed to set up a pop-up PMO?
>
> P3O gives a directive of approximately 10% of the total project lifecycle time. For a one year project you can estimate a bit more than a month for setting up the PMO and all associated project processes.
> It is my experience that in a less mature project organisation and a project manager with little experience in the deployment of PMO employees in the team, this can take longer.

An option is to record all setup tasks in a planning or Excel spreadsheet, in order for you to, as it were, approach the setup of the PMO as a separate subproject.

It can be that, due to limited time and resources, you cannot set up the processes and services in one go. You will prioritise the setting up of the processes and services in close liaison with the project manager.

Sometimes the entire plan and configuration are clear all at once. In the following situations, it is difficult to do this.

6. A POP-UP PMO IN 10 STEPS

- When the project manager has insufficient experience with the idea of project support and pop-up PMO.
- When it is not clear beforehand which processes can be set up and supported.
- When you notice some resistance.

In such cases you apply the salami tactics. Step by step, through iterations (small value-adding steps), you set up the processes and services one by one, as shown in figure 6.1.

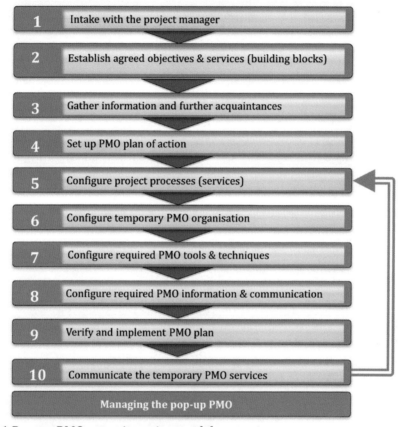

Figure 6.1 Pop-up PMO setup iteration model

6.5 Step 5: Configure project processes (services)

Now you can work out the tasks in detail per process and service.
This can be seen as in depth task descriptions. "Which contacts do you need for which tasks?". "On which days are the agreed reports being published" etc.
In other words: create a guide or manual! Perhaps record any processes in flowcharts and make, if necessary, detailed work instructions.

6. A POP-UP PMO IN 10 STEPS

This will provide for a short training time when a new employee joins the pop-up PMO and ensures transparency in the activities of the PMO. The knowledge is being secured. And that will benefit you next time when setting up a pop-up PMO.

Keep in mind when documenting that a clear distinction should be made between the demands made by the PID or contract and steering committee, and additional requirements of the project manager.
Should there be a change of project manager within the project, this will then not be at the expense of the quality of the activities and the project governance will stay secured.

Also think of matters such as:
- Reaction time (time between submitted application and delivery of the requested) and pre-reaction time (time between taking the initiative and necessary action).
- Continuity in case of long term absence of project manager and PMO employee(s) (sickness, holidays etc.).
- Accountability (to whom) and in what way.
- The capabilities of the PMO (for example developing templates yourself; give solicited and unsolicited advice; hire externals for temporary support; have intake interviews with candidates).
- Quality to be delivered.
- Escalation possibilities.

These are SLA (service level agreement)-like agreements which you can also record in the project manual.

It is very important to point out to the project organisation the set moments within the company processes, so that based on this the meeting schedule of the various business committees can be adjusted. For example, the month consolidation of the financial system, the weekly runs of the time recording system or the budget revision rounds. These processes can be the heartbeat of the project.

6.6 Step 6: Configure the pop-up PMO organisation

It is now possible to assess whether the originally prepared occupancy of the PMO is in line with the services and tasks that are to be carried out. Before you do this, check all possible building blocks (work packages) one last time.
You can now determine the size of the PMO.
- What kind of PMO employees are needed (junior, mid, senior)?
- Are any specialists needed (for example a planner or risk manager)?
- How long for and when are the specialists needed?
- Who is going to control the pop-up PMO as a team (head PMO)?

6. A POP-UP PMO IN 10 STEPS

- How often and when will the alignment between the PMO employees take place?
- How often and when will the alignment between the PMO employee and project manager take place?
- How has replacement been arranged in the absence of PMO support (sickness, holidays, etc.)?
- Are there any mandatory or optional forms to be included?

6.7 Step 7: Configure PMO tools & techniques

From the discussion with the project manager and further discussions in the (line) organisation, you have been able to get an idea of present and necessary tools and techniques.

- What is required and what do you need in addition?
- Which project management methodology is being employed?
- Which templates are available and which ones can you make (or have made)?
- Which software is going to be used and is there sufficient knowledge available of in the PMO team?
- How do you get access to the tools?

6.8 Step 8: Configure PMO information & communication

The pop-up PMO always has an advisory role within the project. You are the central point of the project. Communication to and from the other project employees is of crucial importance. Everyone should know how procedures run and where they can find which templates. The PMO makes these available and checks whether they are being used.
One of the key things that the PMO is going to communicate about are the activities it carries out to support the project and how it can be reached.

You can provide this information via an internal project site (intranet), special project management or other system and/or via a (printed) document. Which is most useful will depend on the situation. If there are people hired from other companies, they usually cannot login immediately and then a printout will be more effective.

Record at least the following information:
- How can the PMO be reached?
    - Mailbox
    - Physical location
    - Telephone
    - Social media

6. A POP-UP PMO IN 10 STEPS

   - SharePoint
   - Other tools
- What are the rights and obligations of the project participants (think of time sheets, sickness, holidays and leave, issue handling etc.)?
- What kind of questions can project employees ask the PMO? Which services does the PMO offer?

> Tip: Create a type of PMO menu (service catalogue) when there are many potential service customers besides the project manager. This prevents having to sell "no" too often.
>
> With a high demand for a particular service that cannot yet be delivered, the menu can always be reconsidered (as long as there is time, expertise, budget and employees available).

6.9 Step 9: Verify and implement PMO plan of action

In step 4 you started setting up the plan of action. Based on the configure steps 5 through 8, you continued filling in the details of the plan.
At the configuration steps you have probably also partly dealt with already formulated action points.
Now check your plan again to see whether you have not forgotten anything and update the status of your action points. Perhaps you can use the "pop-up PMO setup checklist" in appendix D. You will carry out this step after every iteration and it will be a constant process when setting up or amending PMO services.

6.10   Step 10: Communicate the temporary PMO services

From the moment the communication on the pop-up PMO is not powerful enough, in the worst case scenario project employees will go their own way. As a consequence, some of the tasks implemented by the PMO will not provide the desired results. Why keep a list of contacts when nobody knows it is available? Why have team leaders sent a status update when they do not know and see exactly what is being done with it? To provide insight and transparency is the reason why input is requested.
By giving, you can take. In addition there is the advantage that the project employees can better assess where and how a change has impact, whereby they can notify the PMO of this in time.

The best method to properly address this from the start is to, during the kick-off of the project, draw attention to the tasks that the PMO will carry out. Initially, the agreed tasks can be presented within the project processes. From the start the business environment knows what the PMO stands for and what they can expect

6. A POP-UP PMO IN 10 STEPS

from it. Of course there will also be looked at what the PMO expects of the project environment.

Discuss the contents of the presentation beforehand with the project manager. It may be that he or she wants to see more or less focus on certain tasks. The overview of the tasks of the PMO can be distributed or placed on a team site. Once tasks are being added or deleted, the overview will be updated and communicated again.

> *I was once hired by a project manager for various PMO activities. I was the only PMO employee on the project and soon also team leaders came to ask if I wanted to take on certain tasks (services). I was pleased with these requests because they saw the added value of my services. Project team members also came to me with all kinds of questions.*
>
> *Over time, however, it was just too much work for one person and I often had to say no. As a result, everyone was unhappy.*
>
> *I decided to list all my tasks (logically grouped by type of service) and to whom I delivered which services and why. But above all, to whom I could not deliver certain services anymore due to lack of time and how much time those services took up.*
>
> *When I started I was the only PMO employee, after this analysis a separate planner, a report writer, a junior PMO employee and a secretary were added on my request.*
>
> *Together with the team leaders we communicated clearly who could be approached for what via a project newsletter and via the team site. And which tasks the PMO would not perform and one was supposed to do oneself.*
>
> *In short "the PMO menu".*

7. MANAGING THE POP-UP PMO

Projects can always be found in a changing environment. As a result, the needs of the project manager in the project can also be changing. This is independent of the processes that require continuous attention in a project (finances, planning, risk management, issue and change management, configuration and information management, quality management etc.). Within the PMO there should be sufficient capacity available to at least support and manage the agreed processes, so that in any case the "core" of the project continues to run efficiently. Furthermore, there needs to be capacity to support project employees.

Periodically review the collaboration between the temporary PMO employees or the head of the pop-up PMO and the project manager and whether there are still matters that could or should be adjusted.
In the beginning this may be weekly, over time this can be reduced to once every two weeks.

These kind of conversations can also be used to share information that both encountered whilst implementing the processes and to align possible strategies. The more inside information the project manager shares with the PMO, the better it can act.

The one-time staffing of a PMO is not to be taken for granted, because over the course of the project the responsibilities of the pop-up PMO can change. The tasks and the need of the project manager determine the required expertise. A pop-up PMO can temporarily get expertise from a permanent PMO elsewhere in the organisation (provided there is one).

The quality of the collaboration between project manager and PMO and also of the project is being determined, among others, by:
- the extent to which a project manager is not afraid to hand over tasks to the PMO,
- how much he or she is willing to let go,
- the extent to which he or she is open to taking advice from the PMO employee,
- how proactive and assertive the PMO employee is and by the knowledge and experience level of both.

During the project life cycle, PMO tasks may be added or deleted. When tasks are removed or added, certain competences will or will not be necessary.

Betting too low (for example administrative support) on a too big and heavy work package means that the quality will go down. The project manager will not get extra time to pay attention to other matters and will eventually have to do the delegated tasks to a large extent himself or should at least check very closely.

7. MANAGING THE POP-UP PMO

Betting too high (for example quality control) on a too small work package (making a plan) will lead to frustration of the PMO employee and possibly even to competitive behaviour (competition with the project manager). Intentionally or unintentionally, the PMO employee will form his opinion on the activities of the project manager and will also express this. After all, managing a project/programme is also his or her expertise, more so than, for example, making a plan. This can lead to 2 captains that will possibly sink the ship.

Beforehand, one should really have thought about the contents of the task packages. Accordingly, with the job description a (function) profile can be drawn up. It is quite possible that the various tasks do not fit into one profile. Do not try to (so-called) weigh down or lighten the task package so as to make it fit into one profile; ultimately, you will not reach your goal because of it. Once the profile has been drawn up, you can determine whether it should be a full-time or a part-time resource.

As already mentioned, needs can change gradually. It is therefore important to also periodically pay attention to the overview of time spent and to keep this as up to date as possible. It is possible that for example for a certain period more attention to planning is needed (at the transition of a phase) so that more hours are being spent on it and perhaps an extra employee is temporarily required.
Activities can occur:
- Daily (e.g. dealing with issues).
- Weekly (e.g. make a progress report).
- Monthly (e.g. approve timesheets).
- Per project (e.g. one-off setup).
- Yearly (e.g. budgeting).
- Ad hoc (e.g. an escalation).

In order to get a better insight into the possible work package of a pop-up PMO, the building blocks as described in the following two chapters can be consulted. What this could mean to time spent will be further discussed in chapter 12 "Size matters. How many are needed for the PMO?".

7. MANAGING THE POP-UP PMO

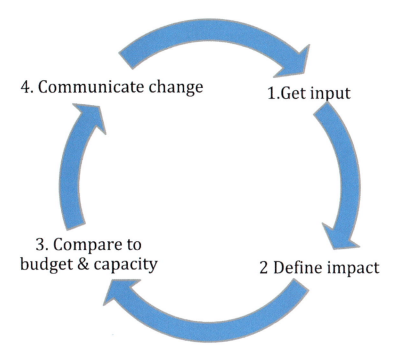

Figure 7.1 Types of PMO tasks and utilisation cycle

The above figure shows a cycle that aims to align the time spent of the PMO period with the needs of the environment and the finance controller. Such a cycle ensures that the PMO can justify its capacity need.
1. In response to a trigger from outside the project or a self-assessment it has become apparent that the time spent should be revised.
2. It is to be determined whether this change has such an impact that the staffing of the PMO should be changed.
3. If the staffing of the PMO is to be changed, the change in the aspect of budget will be discussed with the project manager before it is being implemented. And after possible agreement elsewhere in the projects or line organisation.
4. The change in tasks, division of tasks or staffing will be communicated to the environment.

This cycle will have to re-run in a number of cases.
1. <u>A new project manager is being appointed:</u> The pop-up PMO will have a meeting with the new project manager. Here, the PMO will mention in what tasks it is engaged and wherein support is being offered to the project. During this meeting the expectations of the new project manager are being discussed and whether he or she has additional requirements.
2. <u>A big change is taking place in the environment of the project or an important phase is being completed:</u> The environment of the programme is changing in such a way that it is expected that the pop-up PMO will have to spend its time differently. An example is the period in which a transition of

7. MANAGING THE POP-UP PMO

phase to another is taking place. During this period, large amounts of project products will have to be signed off on and new products will have to be scheduled. More capacity is needed then. Another example is that when setting up the PMO at the start of the project, more senior PMO officers are being employed. Once the pop-up PMO has been set up, the work will be handed over to junior or mid-level PMO employees if the weight of the task package allows it.

3. <u>A periodic assessment/work meeting will be held:</u> For example, the pop-up PMO will hold biweekly work meetings with the project manager. For this meeting the PMO employee checks whether the time spent is still reflecting the current situation. Major changes/details can be discussed. During this meeting the project manager will receive the opportunity to indicate that specific tasks require a higher priority.

Managing a PMO is balancing between processes and people. It can be counterproductive to flood people with too much method and process, hence finding the right mix for the pop-up PMO is essential. To achieve this, we must focus on the five P's for PMO[5]:

- People. Recruitment, profiles, training, coaching, certification, assessment and teambuilding.
- Process. Methods, quality assurance, assessment and authority.
- Performance. Profiling of projects, project reporting, dashboard, key performance indicators (KPIs), budget and escalation paths.
- Promotion. Internal and external communication, marketing and success stories.
- Project Management Information Systems (PMIS) (tools).

Who manages the PMO employees in the pop-up PMO?

Depending on how the pop-up PMO is organised and of how many people it consists, there are several variations possible.

With a pop-up PMO of 1 or 2 people the project manager is the (temporary) manager of these employees. When there are more PMO employees, the project manager can delegate this to a head PMO.
This is not always apparent, in figure 7.2 I outline a number of situations that I have come across.

---

[5] Leading successful PMOs, Peter Taylor

7. MANAGING THE POP-UP PMO

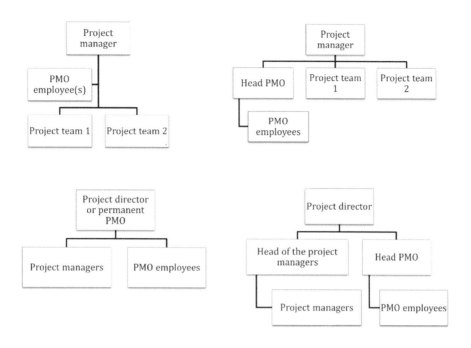

Figure 7.2 Examples of PMO employee management

A pop-up PMO can be managed by the project manager, a permanent PMO or a project director. The PMO employees can be managed by the project manager, a permanent PMO, project director or a head PMO.

8. BUILDING BLOCKS: PROJECT PROCESSES (FUNCTIONS & SERVICES)

Whoever wants to reach a distant goal must take small steps.
Saul Bellow

Just like there are agreements in tasks and processes between a pop-up shop and a permanent store, PMO tasks and processes can also be applied to different types of PMOs. Again, the differences between a pop-up PMO and a permanent PMO are the temporary character, the mostly very short setup time, a new location and a new project steering team (project management and support).

In this book I combine the IPMA-PMO tasks and the P3O services and functions into possible services or building blocks of the pop-up PMO. The pop-up PMO can offer these services to a project or programme. Below is an overview from which you can choose, equipped with a brief description. These services (building blocks) will be discussed in further detail in chapter 9 and 10.

Objective of a service: Planning

Chapter	P3O service	IPMA-PMO Task/work package	Description
N/A	Portfolio build, prioritisation, analysis and reporting		*As P3O and MoP mean it, this is covered by a Portfolio office, not within a project or programme.*
9.1	Programme and project set-up & closure		The first matter to be arranged once the project has been identified and mandated. Hand over the project file to the line organisation or permanent PMO at the end of the project. Phase out facilities and access rights.
9.2	Stakeholder engagement & communications	Communication management Stakeholder management	Supporting the most effective way of communication with all stakeholders of the project.

8. BUILDING BLOCKS: PROJECT PROCESSES (FUNCTIONS & SERVICES)

Chapter	P3O service	IPMA-PMO Task/work package	Description
9.3	Planning and estimating	Planning	Facilitating an up to date schedule including dependencies and checking progress.
9.4	Capacity planning & resource management	Resource management	Facilitating that the right people and means are available at the right time.
9.5	Benefit management	Benefit management	Identifying, quantifying, realising, controlling and monitoring the benefits.
N/A	Performance monitoring	*Is often seen at permanent PMO level, not within a project, although it could also take place there.*	Establishing and monitoring the programme or project performance indicators KPIs. Improve project performances (optimising).

Objective of a service: Delivery

Chapter	P3O service	IPMA-PMO Task/work package	Description
N/A	Monitoring & review	*Is often seen at permanent PMO level, not within a project.*	Continue monitoring and periodic reviews of all project processes and plans. Give solicited and unsolicited advice.
10.1	Reporting	Reporting	Collecting and analysing data and information. Edit and aggregate them into management reports.
10.2	Risk management	Risk management	Identifying, recording and monitoring of risks and countermeasures. Facilitate risk workshop.
10.3	Issue management	Issue management	Make sure that issues are being identified and recorded. Monitoring progress with respect to resolving issues or escalations.

8. BUILDING BLOCKS: PROJECT PROCESSES (FUNCTIONS & SERVICES)

Chapter	P3O service	IPMA-PMO Task/work package	Description
10.4	Change control	Change management	Identifying, recording and monitoring of changes. Facilitate project Change Advisory Board (CAB).
10.5	Finance	Project finances	Forecasting and monitoring the project finances. Facilitate the project in order to be and to stay financially in control.
N/A	Commercial (including supplier management)	*Is often seen at permanent PMO level, not within a project.*	Coordinating with purchasing department and other commercial departments in order to buy products and services at favourable prices.
10.6	Quality assurance	Quality management	Monitoring that the project and the project results meet the requirements, needs and expectations. Participate in audits.
10.7	Information, configuration and asset management	Information and configuration management	The managing and monitoring of all project information and data (repositories). Baseline, project products and file monitoring.
10.8	Transition management		Assist business change managers in transitions. Facilitate handover to management (the operation).
10.10	Secretariat		Relieving the project organisation with regard to organising and reporting appointments, meetings and gatherings. Organise facility matters.

8. BUILDING BLOCKS: PROJECT PROCESSES (FUNCTIONS & SERVICES)

Objective of a service: Centre of Excellence (CoE)

Chapter	P3O service	IPMA-PMO Task/work package	Description
N/A	Standards & methods (processes & tools)	*If a CoE is present, then the pop-up PMO will maintain contact with the CoE and apply the available standards. Are certain templates & standards missing, the pop-up PMO will then develop these for the benefit of the project.*	Consistent with existing processes and templates of an organisation. Setting up and communicating project standards. Is often seen at permanent PMO level, not within a project.
N/A	Internal consultancy	*Is often seen at permanent PMO level. Within a project it is the advising of the project manager.*	
10.9	Organisational learning and knowledge management	Knowledge management	Bring, share and take from lessons learned at other projects/programmes.
N/A	People & skills	*Is often seen at permanent PMO level, not within a project.*	Identify competences and need for knowledge (or lack of). Observe the projects and take action if necessary.

In the following chapters, we are working from a combination of the IPMA-PMO Special Interest Group and P3O format.

8. BUILDING BLOCKS: PROJECT PROCESSES (FUNCTIONS & SERVICES)

Figure 8.1 Pop-Up PMO building blocks

In accordance to P3O a division has been made between the planning (chapter 9) and delivery (chapter 10) building blocks (functions and services).

8.1 Clarification to the paragraphs in chapter 9 and 10

Hereafter, every project process (functions and services) discussed will be explained in detail according to a set format in the following chapters. Every process can be set up in the pop-up PMO as a possible building block.
- Objective.
- Which stakeholders are involved.
- What can the PMO do at setup.
- Controlled progress by the PMO.
- Techniques and tools to be used.
- Risks when the process is not set up properly.

> **In this coloured block you will find an example of the service concerned, with setting up a pop-up shop as the metaphor.**

Which stakeholders are involved in this service?
Who do you need in order to set this process up properly? Besides of course the project manager, the project team and, possibly already present in the organisation, a permanent PMO. In other words, these are the "PMO stakeholders".

8. BUILDING BLOCKS: PROJECT PROCESSES (FUNCTIONS & SERVICES)

What can the PMO do at setup?

Activities necessary to set up this process (what can you organise). What the PMO does depends on, among others, the capacity and experience of the PMO employee(s) and on what the project manager does personally or wants to delegate the possible tasks and activities are in random order.

Controlled progress by the PMO

Which activities have to/can take place during the project when the process has been set up? The possible tasks and activities are in random order.

Techniques and tools to be used

Which tools can you use? Several options are being mentioned, they do not all have to be used. There are probably still more.

For every building block (process), templates and possible software systems are a probable tool. As well as various project and programme management methodologies, including:

- DSDM Atern V2 (the successor of Dynamic Systems Development Method (DSDM)),
- Managing Successful Programmes (MSP),
- New Product Development (NPD),
- Project Management Body of Knowledge (PMBOK),
- Projects IN Controlled Environment (PRINCE2),
- Process management,
- Project Driven Creation/"Projectmatig Creëren" (PMC),
- Agile and Scrum,
- Systems Engineering.

These are therefore not further specified in the elaboration per building block in the following chapters and paragraphs.

Risks

What risks does one run when this service is not being set up properly. This is an indication and is certainly not complete.

Of all these building blocks you need to know the following:
- Who will implement the service and possibly set up?
- What are the process agreements?
- Where can I find the information?

N.B. it does not matter whether the pop-up PMO, the project manager or a staff organisation delivers and implements a building block, as long as it is organised and is clear. As a PMO employee you should see to the clarification and securing of this within the project.

First take on before you continue on.
The court jester

9. BUILDING BLOCKS: PLANNING

9.1 Project set-up & closure

Objective:
The first matters that need to be organised when the project is identified and has a mandate.

> A perfumery chain wants to, for the promotion of a new fragrance, open a pop-up shop in the centre of a big city for 1 month. A project manager has been appointed, supported by a PMO employee. All kinds of facilities need to be organised like a temporary location, store supplies, a cash register and shop personnel.
> And when the shop closes up, these kind of matters need to be dissolved again of course. A good job for a PMO employee. With the pop-up shop roadmap (setup checklist) this is all quickly organised, including the matters that the holding has forgotten about, like the telephone and internet connection.

Which stakeholders are involved in this service?
- Project manager.
- Facility services.
- ICT service department.
- Permanent PMO.

What can the PMO do at setup?
- Retrieve frameworks, guidelines, templates, pop-up PMO configuration script and other tools for the permanent PMO.
- Organise facility services like accesses to locations, systems, applications.
- Draw project organisation chart.
- Apply for and set up central project mailbox.
- Build list of contacts involved, with e-mail address, telephone number, location, organisation name, stakeholder group name (stakeholder register).
- Collect templates, adjust them for the project and communicate to team members.
- Organise kick-off.
- Establish project rules.
- Build project file structure and location(s).
- See to it that the project governance is clear and known to everyone.
- Look for lessons learned from similar projects.

9.1. Project set up & closure

Controlled progress
- Maintain information.
- Facilitate on and offboarding of employees (see resource management).
- Prepare next workshops.
- Set next services setup in motion.
- Make appointments with suppliers and PMO stakeholders (these are the stakeholders involved with a certain PMO service, i.e. building block).
- Adjust templates due to organisational changes or because of lessons learned.

What can the PMO do when closing the project?
- Collect and distribute the lessons learned.
- Handover and/or archive the administrative documents.
- Return the office facilities.
- Cancel rights and authorities.
- Terminate contracts with contractors and suppliers.
- Finalise all financial transactions and update the final costs.
- Hold a final project meeting.
- Release personnel capacities and other assets.
- Draft discharge form and add signed version to the project file.
- Archive project file.
- Distribute the final report.

Techniques and tools to be used
- (Digital) photo wall of the project participants.
- Project team kick-off.
- Workshops like a Project Start Up (PSU).

Risks
If this service is not being set up properly, then one runs the following risks:
- All project employees lose a lot of time on research (higher project costs).
- Everyone is trying to reinvent the wheel themselves.
- There is insufficient insight in the project governance.

9.1. Project set up & closure

For the process not to be reliant on one person, it is recommended to run all project communication via a central mailbox. When PMO employees change, the desk will stay unchanged and people can collectively work from the mailbox. Transfer of work between colleagues has a low threshold which benefits the cooperation. A central mailbox also increases the visibility and accessibility.

Example agenda of a PSU or kick-off day(s) with the project team:
- Kick-off by the client (explanation project objectives and expected benefits).
- Get acquainted (interactive with a team building element).
- Present or set up project organisation (link with organisation, steering committee, (sub) project leaders, roles and responsibilities).
- Determine scope of the project (what and what not) and expected products.
- Develop Product Breakdown Structure (PBS) or Work Breakdown Structure (WBS) and planning.
- Force field analysis.
- Risk analysis.
- Presentation(s) by project team(s) to client, record actions and decisions.

It drove me mad to tell the 3rd new project employee again what the URL of the intranet site was, how to book a meeting room, what the address of the printer was or when you needed to register your hours in the time registration system. This was costing me too much time. With the 4th new project employee I had a "welcome new project employee" document with all such basic and useful information ready.

9.1. Project set up & closure

Everything comes to an end sometime

It is probably a bit strange to, already at the beginning of this book, talk about closing the project and the pop-up PMO. However, everything that you set up for a temporary organisation like a project, you will most likely also have to break down and dismantle. This is one of the distinctive characteristics of a pop-up PMO.

There will always be a time that a project or a programme comes to its end. This can be in accordance to planning with the desired products and/or results delivered, or it can be forced because, for example, the original assignment has been changed or the necessary financial coverage has fallen through. Whatever the reason may be, the activities of the pop-up PMO are no longer required for the support of the project or programme.

What then are the closing activities of a pop-up PMO?
This is usually limited to burning the project or programme documentation onto a CD-ROM and facilitate a lessons learned sessie (see chapter 10.9 "Knowledge management"). The PMO is also implicitly being discharged in the discharge form. A final calculation is being done and a final check whether all invoices and timesheets have gone out. The lights can be switched off, a final e-mail message sent out and on to the next assignment.

Every project and programme has a closing phase. Within PRINCE2 and MSP we know the phases "Closing a Project" and "Closing a Program". PMBOK talks about "End project with closing processes". In the Atern method they speak of "Deployment" and in the Dutch A4 project method this is being tackled in the fourth quadrant (completion).
In all these phases the transfer of the pop-up PMO activities from the project/programme organisation to the line organisation is a component, however, it is usually not named so explicitly. Please note, I do not mean the project product results, these will be covered in transition management.

Everything that is being managed and recorded by a PMO and the project manager has to be transferred to the line organisation or to a permanent PMO and/or the control organisation.
Appendix E contains a checklist to help with what can be transferred to whom and which activities need to be implemented by the PMO in order to dissolve itself.

9.1. Project set up & closure

At the closing of a programme I discovered that even though the projects within the programme were indeed closed for time writing, the projects in the financial system were still fully open.
Only then it became clear how it was that every month there was an unexplainable difference between the registrations in the budgets and the actual expenditure of the programme. In the financial system, invoices just continued being booked on projects that were not visible anymore in the operational finances (and reports).
This shows again the importance of properly closing projects and transferring outstanding cost carriers to (in this case) the programme manager.

(Wijnand)

The closing of a project can, for some project members, be an emotional happening.
Besides the official process of closing a project, there should be space and time for an informal goodbye to each other.
For example, go for a bite to eat or drink together somewhere, possibly preceded by a lessons learned or evaluation session.

Communication is often the biggest problem of the solution.
Hein Pragt

 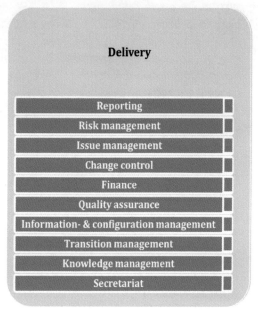

9.2 Stakeholder management and communication

Objective:
Supporting the most effective way of communicating with all stakeholders of the project.
Through good stakeholder management, the chance of a successful succeeding of the project increases, because through good analysis and communication you know who and how to consult, instruct or inform.

> **It should be researched who are all involved in setting up the pop-up shop and what the interests are of these groups of people.**
>
> **The PMO employee discovers that the client has an accountant who needs to be consulted and that there is a possibility to quickly hire project employees via a special agency. The PMO employee also discovers that in the week that the pop-up shop is to go live, there is an event on for which a special newspaper is being made. Perhaps a piece on the pop-up shop can be placed in it?**

Which stakeholders are involved in setting up this service?
- Project managers and employees.
- Communication department.
- Journalists.
- IT department.

What can the PMO do at setup?
- Help develop a shared vision on or mission for the project in the plans.
- Set up communication plan.
- Determine communication strategy and target group approach.
- Facilitate meetings and workshops with project stakeholders.
- Set up stakeholder folder and overview.
- Develop stakeholder profiles.
- Facilitate in formulation of stakeholder engagement strategy.
- Set up project intranet site (or portal).
- Set up activity calendar.
- Facilitate a Product Owner training.

Controlled progress
- Maintain stakeholder folder and overview.
- Coordinate stakeholder and progress meetings.
- Advise the project manager in determining the communication strategy, target group approach, stakeholder management and identified resistors.
- Implement, execute and control the communication plan.

9.2. Stakeholder management and communication

- Provide internal newsletters (to project team and BAU).
- Ensure timely communication to involved employees and management.
- Take care of external communication (possibly with communication department).
- Be a central point of communication and handle information requests.
- Maintain project intranet site (or portal).
- Measure/monitor effectiveness of the communication.
- Take away possible barriers between the Agile team and the organisation.

Techniques and tools to be used
- Collaborate portal tools like intranet, internet tools.
- Communication plan.
- RACI matrix. Overview to list the roles and responsibilities of the people involved in the project or BAU activities (Responsible, Accountable, Consulted, Informed).
- Stakeholder engagement strategy.
- Stakeholder folders or force field analysis.
- Stakeholder profiles.

Risks
If this service is not being set up properly, then one runs the following risks:
- Resistance to change.
- Wrong expectations of the outcome.
- Lots of noise in and around the project.
- Misinterpretations due to a lack of consistent usage in terminology.

For a large project at a government agency, I was appointed as communication manager. I came in contact with a specialist journal that wanted to dedicate 3 articles to this project. I thought, a great opportunity for "free publicity" for the company that was hired to do the job. After consultation with some key internal stakeholders it was decided not to cooperate on the three publications. These were therefore not carried out. Fortunately, because the project did not always run as smooth and could have received negative publicity due to the publications. Communication is also sometimes deciding not to communicate, however much you wanted it too.

Don't forget the PMO communication and promotion. What is the added value of the PMO? What are the PMO services (building blocks)? What are success stories of you PMO.

9.2. Stakeholder management and communication

Communication is the key factor to get support and information

As a communication specialist in the pop-up PMO you need to take care that it is not being automatically assumed that you will therefore organise everything in this area of expertise. Your primary task is mapping what is needed, in order to put the involved project manager and stakeholders to work. You facilitate the necessary contacts and meetings at a structural way.

Stakeholders are people involved who are affected positively or negatively by the project. You need to know who the stakeholders are and what their interests are before you can start making a communication plan.
The identification of the way in which stakeholders can influence the project or are being influenced and what their attitude is towards the project objective is being described in a stakeholder analysis.

Steps in the stakeholder analysis process:
1. Identify the stakeholders. This can be through a brainstorm session. Create a sort of mind map.

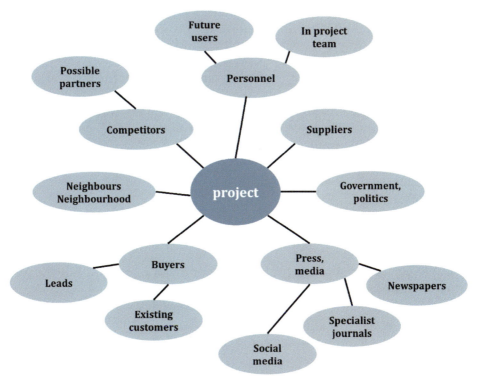

Figure 9.1 Identifying stakeholders

2. Understand the interests of the stakeholders and map them on characteristics and classifications. For example positive, supporting, passive negative, opposing, neutral, unknown. You can do this at high level (total) or

9.2. Stakeholder management and communication

you can zoom in on individuals per stakeholder group. You summarise this in a stakeholder matrix like below.

Stakeholders	Characteristics • Socio-economic • Diversity (opportunities groups) • Structure, organisation, status • Behaviour	Interests and expectations • Interests, objectives • Expectations	Sensitivity and respect for • Horizontal themes • Diversity	Potential and limitations • Resources/means • Knowledge, experience, skills • Potential contribution to project	Consequences and decisions for the project • Which action • How to deal with the group
Stakeholder 1					
Stakeholder 2					
Stakeholder 3					

3. Finally, map the relations between (individual) stakeholders. Who have a good or rather bad relationship with each other.

As a project team you do a stakeholder analysis behind closed doors. Everyone should feel at liberty to give his or her opinion. To describe someone's attitude towards the change may be a sensitive matter. It is useful to often repeat an analysis session during the project. Opinions of people can change over time or something within the project changes resulting in different interests for the people involved.

In addition, it is important to find out from the client the interest and objective of the project and possible change. With a bit of luck there is a well written business case, even then it is still useful to ask the client the following questions[6]:

- What does this change add to the organisation objectives and strategy?
- What happens when we will not do it?
- What will be different later?
- What is it REALLY about?
- Who cares? Who has got an interest?
- Who will notice anything?
- How would you describe the project to your mother or aunt on a birthday?
- What do your employees think of it, you think?
- What would you like to know from your employees?
- What is the doom scenario?

Do not be surprised if there are vague answers, keep asking until everything is clear. If the client cannot make it clear themselves, why would you be able to then? After all, it is their project, right?

---

[6] Monica Wigman "Regel jij het draagvlak?" ("Will you organise the baseline?" Only available in Dutch)

9.2. Stakeholder management and communication

Do not forget the importance of internal project team communication. In the delusion and momentum of the day, especially in large projects with multiple teams, it is sometimes being forgotten to communicate progress or decisions within the project and to celebrate milestones.
Possible options are:
- Internal project newsletter.
- Soapbox session.
- Team site with a sort of project logbook (blogs) that every team member can add to.
- A physical or digital planning board or scrum board.
- Interim evaluations.
- Social media (LinkedIn group, Yammer, etc.).

In a certain project there were a lot of planned communication activities. Just like the planned meetings, I had scheduled them as an appointment in the shared calendar of the PMO mailbox. Should I unexpectedly not be there, my colleague could see what needed to be done.

The biggest challenge of today is the great selection of possible media to use.
Offline like posters, USB sticks, printed M&Ms, roadshows.
Online like e-mails, blogs, video, text messages, Twitter, Facebook.
The right choice of media requires clarity about the objectives, the message to be communicated, and most of all understanding the target group.

Nobody gets lost on a straight path.
(Goethe)

9.3 Planning

Objective:
Facilitate an up-to-date schedule including dependencies and check progress.

> To soon be able to start with building the pop-up shop, the PMO employee is asked to think about setting up a schedule and to keep this up to date. The PMO employee organises a kick-off with the team and facilitates that, at the end of the day, there is a logical overview of the work to be done. It has also become clear when the final results have to be delivered and what possible dependencies are.

Which stakeholders are involved in setting up this service?
- The project team including architects and specialists.
- Everyone involved in the project and especially those who are going to deliver, build or execute something.

What can the PMO do at setup?
- Give advice on the structure of the schedule and sub schedules to project manager (agree on standard). The rolling up from detail to high level schedule should be as simple as possible.
- Consolidate high level schedule based on the detail schedules of the teams.
- Create a project roadmap.
- Estimate impact of project schedule in regards to the operational plans/planning.
- Make product and subsequently work breakdown structure (WBS).
- Arrange naming convention for product names (for tips see also information and configuration management).
- Establish and review work packages.
- Import schedule in planning tool.
- Identify dependencies in the schedule.
- Analyse and advise about critical path.

Controlled progress
- Maintain/actualise the schedule and roadmap.
- Take initiatives for the improvement of the schedule and planning process.
- Address the team members on milestones and products from the schedule.
- Monitor, maintain and sustain dependencies.
- Review adjusted schedules.
- When changes have occurred, update the schedule(s).
- Monitor the velocity with Agile. Signal and alarm when the velocity is at risk.
- Drive to reduction of 'work in progress' (in Agile terms: backlog size).
- Take care of the iteration reviews.

9.3 Planning

Techniques and tools to be used
- Agile planning model.
- Atomising[7] (from the Gamestorming book).
- Bang-for-Buck. A scrum technique used for the prioritisation of tasks.
- Critical Chain planning (Goldratt).
- Planning poker (scrum).
- Planning tools (several suppliers).
- Organise and direct planning workshop.
- Product-based planning.
- Product Breakdown Structure (PBS) and Work Breakdown Structure (WBS).
- Product flow diagram. A flow chart of the in the PBS named products containing dependencies between products and the logical order in which it is being delivered.

Risks
If this service is not being set up properly, then one runs the following risks:
- No up-to-date schedule.
- Sub schedules are not aligned to one another.
- No monitoring and control of project possible.
- Time overflow of the project.
- Expected costs of the project are not easy to monitor and forecast.
- Resource management is only partly possible.

Once, a project manager was a bit pressed for time to deliver his plan of action and schedule for a restart of a large and complex project at a client. I was asked to temporarily help out and import the schedule into MS Project, in short an ad hoc planning job.

Whilst going through and discussing the schedule and filling in the tool, I proposed to also take up in the schedule the progress reports, meetings and steering committee meetings. The project manager agreed with it, which he normally never did.

After also having included this information in the schedule, it showed that:
- *Delivery of products, reports and decision-making were not aligned to one another,*
- *The time it took to write the report was not taken into account,*
- *No account was taken of the fact that the steering committee wanted the parts a week in advance in order to read them through.*

Subsequently, the project manager took up resource planning in his budget, and a PMO employee (m/f) in the team.

(Mark)

---

[7] Gamestorming: A Playbook for Innovators, Rulebreakers, and Changemakers, Dave Gray, Sunni Brown and James Macanufo

9.3 Planning

If you are failing to plan, then you are planning to fail

There is a saying "Every minute you spend planning will save you 10 minutes in execution". The cost recovery model of the time you spend on planning will soon be clear then. With projects that are still to be sold to a client and for which fixed price agreements are being made, it is likely that the below mentioned steps have already been put in the proposal phase. In what other way can you get a good calculation? Nevertheless, there are more and more organisations that plan according to iterations and embrace the Agile way of thinking. Agile planning is explained further in process 2.

Process 1: Planning according to waterfall method: In 5 steps from global plan to planning

Step 1: You need to look back in order to start
The making of a plan starts at retrieving of and searching for previous lessons learned. Is what had to be done or made ever done before? If so, what were the lessons learned? In short "Use your lessons learned!" You can probably find these in a database, site or other form of storage within or outside your organisation. Or by asking questions to a colleague.
Also consider which planning methodology fits the type of project and organisation. Building a bridge differs from developing an application. Do you choose the detailed waterfall or the Agile methodology?

Step 2: Plan the planning
If you want to make sure that you have, as far as time goes, finished 10% sooner or not go over time, you need to at least devote 10% of the project control time to maintaining the schedule.
You can also make the mentioned steps clear in a planning workshop, in order to utilise all available knowledge and to agree with each other on who monitors the plan(s) and updates when necessary.

Project planning is not only the job of the project manager or PMO employee, all stakeholders need to be involved. Because of this you create commitment and a baseline platform. The plan will become realistic and through involvement achievable.

Step 3: Bite sized chunks and process agreements
Next, you think about which products need to be delivered. A product can be tangible, or can also be a service, a software application or documents. Then you continue subdividing the products step by step into logical sub products. In short, make a PBS (Product Breakdown Structure). The PBS can be a bullet list.

9.3 Planning

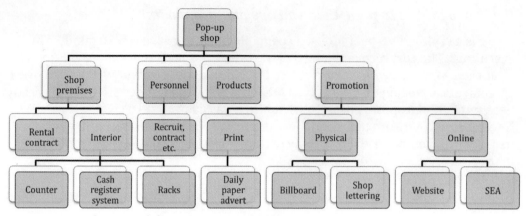

Figure 9.2 Product Breakdown Structure (PBS)

If there are multiple project teams (with their own schedule), naming conventions and dependencies should be arranged. Further:
- Who will maintain the schedule?
- How will this be rolled up into an aggregated schedule?
- In what way are changes on the team schedules being communicated?

The type of project and the organisation determine the detail of the aggregated schedule.

Step 4: Time is money
Only when the structure and the planning process are clear, you will come around to the time factor.
- How long will it take to make the (sub) products?
- Which operations and activities are needed for that?
- What should be done when, what is the order (product flow diagram)?
- What is a logical phasing?
- What are the most important milestones?
- Which releases and iterations?

The product descriptions can be elaborated. These should be brief and to the point. We now come to an ever finer basis for a good calculation and planning. See what you do in which phase.

Set up your baseline. In the first baseline you determine when which sub product is to be delivered and also when which costs are being made. This is also the foundation for Earned Value Analysis (EVA). Earned Value Analysis is a method to determine the progress of a project and to forecast what the actual costs and the final end date will be. Based on the planning data, the time spent and the executed budget, at a certain moment of measurement (x) it is being calculated how much value has already been earned by the project (earned value). The application of EVA can only work in a project organisation if:

9.3 Planning

- Requirements are defined and agreed with the client.
- Product Breakdown Structure (PBS), planning and budget are complete, clear and baselined (client agrees).
- Change management process has been set up and every scope, time or quality change follows this process.
- Everybody is clear on what percentage ready means. When is 100% ready also actually ready. Is that including tests and client agreement? What are the agreed benchmarks for other percentages?
- You have sufficient understanding of the exploitation of costs.
- There is no pressure from the client on the project results. There should be transparency and trust. There should be no fear when bringing bad news.

Of the classic devil's triangle scope, time and cost, the "time" factor is in a large proportion of the projects the most important to steer at and to realise. Are you running behind in terms of time, it will then cost, in 9 out of 10 cases, more money and the circumstances and requirements might have become obsolete, so the quality delivered no longer meets the needs.

To get a better grip on the quality aspect, the 'iron square' is being used, in which quality has been added as a fourth dimension. After all, when you need to/may deliver the same scope in more time and with more money, this will benefit the quality of the product.

N.B. the scope stands for the limitations of the total of the to be delivered products, services and to be carried out activities.

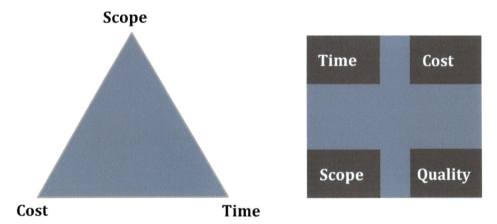

Figure 9.3 The classic devil's triangle and iron square

Step 5 A schedule is already outdated as soon as it is written down.
Establishing a schedule once is doable, the challenge is especially in keeping the schedule up to date.
The PMO employee needs input and information regularly from project and team leaders in order to update the schedule.
Use progress reports, minutes, issue registers and discussions for input. Improve the schedule by sharing it with the complete project team and ask for feedback.

9.3 Planning

A handy tool is to keep a register of all planning issues that you encounter. This is a "planning learned lessons" document that helps to improve the quality of the current schedule and of the planning process for future projects.

Process 2: Planning through iterations

Projects are, despite all our experience in the field of project management and all our training and methodologies, regularly delivered too late and for a higher cost than budgeted, and then the obtained result does not meet either.
Agile approaches, like Scrum or Kanban, take into account the fact that changes move so fast that you can never plan ahead more than four weeks in detail. The prediction is that the rate of change will only increase over the coming years.
Even though these methodologies have been developed for software development projects, they also appear to be very suitable for many types of other projects. Even building a house can be realised using Scrum.

With an Agile (flexible) way of planning, you will already see results within several weeks (maximum 4) and thus deliver value to the business.
Step by step, with continuous feedback from the client, in several short iterations, i.e. 'sprints', the product will be developed. Functionality that the client finds most valuable is delivered first, immediately as a working product. As if you have already gained access to the living room of a house under construction, after which you sprint on to realising the kitchen.

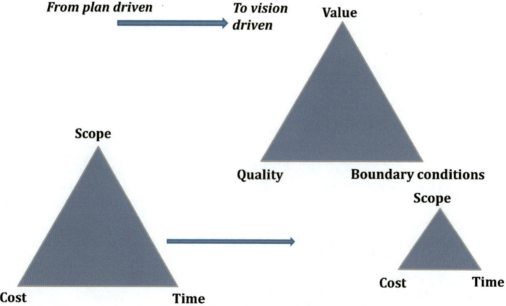

Figure 9.4 From classic devil's triangle to the added value of Agile.

9.3 Planning

In the Agile philosophy a project is successful when it delivers value to the organisation with the expected quality and in accordance to the agreed conditions. Agile determines costs, quality and planning and keeps the scope variable. Not the schedule is leading, but the many value creations in short terms.

The schedule consists of product backlog items and instead of product descriptions, uses user stories.
The product backlog is a list of remaining work for the product. All product backlog items are calculated with business value. This indicates how much value an item has for the client or user. The team equips the items with an estimation. Based on the expected value and effort required, the Return On Investment (ROI) can be calculated. The product backlog is prioritised based on the ROI.
A backlog is only being worked out in detail at the beginning of a sprint. A team will determine the distribution of the work themselves, there is no manager who does this. In practice, self-managing teams turn out to actually have added value.

With an Agile approach like Scrum, there is basically no project manager role. However, there is a product owner. Even though you can still come across the project or programme manager in complex projects with many stakeholders or programmes. The environment and the contract are to be managed and this happens outside the Scrum team, because this team is primarily focused on the delivery of the products.
The role of PMO employee does not exist in Agile. However, when you have a look at the role and competences of a Scrum-master, you see a lot of similarities.
A Scrum-master has a facilitating and coaching role, removes obstacles and ensures the proper execution of the Scrum guidelines.
In addition, a person should look after matters like benefit management, risk management, resource management, communication, knowledge management etc. and there seems to be a task for the PMO in place.

The Product Breakdown Structure (PBS), known from PRINCE2, is the spine of every project. Originally, this tool has especially been used in construction and is a very useful tool. It is perfectly suited for every type of project.

A PBS:
- Makes the scope clear.
- Ensures that sub schedules are better aligned to one another.
- Ensures consistency in the (internal) communication.
- Is the basis of quality control and input for a quality register (see quality management).
- Is the basis for the calculations and controlling of the costs.
- Ensures that risks can easily be assessed and controlled.
- Provides the organisation with clarity on what the project will deliver.

Most organisations staff their problems and starve their opportunities.
Peter Drucker

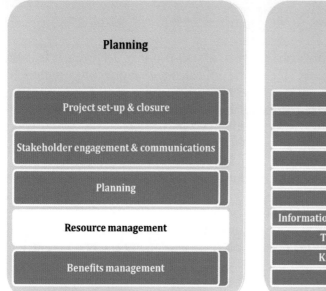
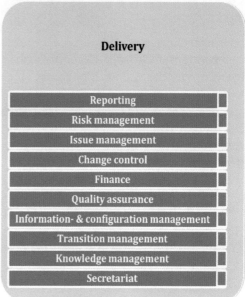

9.4 Resource management

Objective:
Facilitate that the right people and means are available at the right time.

> The PMO employee maps out which skills are required for the shop and manages the first possible candidates. All contracts are being drafted after approval from the project manager.
> Once new employees start working in the shop, they will be helped on their way and trained in the shortest possible time. An extra training will be organised in regards to the new alarm system for, for example, the security employee.
> The required stock of perfume and promotional flyers will be inventoried and recorded in a register.

Which stakeholders are involved in setting up this service?
- HR department.
- Delivery manager.
- Suppliers of personnel (hire) and means.
- Procurement department (internal).
- Facility management.

What can the PMO do at setup?
- Set up an employee resource register (contract lead time, negotiated rates, deployed in which team, from which supplier/department is the resource derived).
- Set up resource register (which buildings, locations, systems, materials are needed at which moment in accordance to which agreements).
- Make agreements with involved stakeholders about how the process should run regarding the recruitment or contracts.
- Establish resourcing requirement (profiles) (draw up or retrieve).
- Create a budget/resource prognosis.

Controlled progress
- Maintain resource register(s).
- Take action proactively when contracts are likely to expire.
- Deploy or have other contracts dissolve if necessary.
- Signal and report bottlenecks (quality, capacity, timeliness, costs).
- Compare incoming invoices with contracts, tenders, scheduled capacity and or approved hours.
- Advice the project manager of fitting solutions in regards to hiring, contracts and financial control.
- Organise resources (set out capacity requests, collect CVs, draw up a shortlist of possible candidates).

9.4 Resource management

- Organise means (buildings, locations, systems, materials).
- Assist with the evaluations of project employees (supply input) and means.
- Maintain and monitor a budget/resource prognosis.

Techniques and tools to be used
- LinkedIn or other business social media tools.
- Resource/skills database (to consult).
- Standard job descriptions (profile templates).
- Inventory administration system.

Risks
If this service is not being set up properly, then one runs the following risks:
- Resources suddenly not deployable anymore to the project.
- Waste.
- Not knowing which suppliers are involved.
- Conflicts over rates and deployment agreements.

> *Whether it belongs to the chapter planning or resource management, having all employees maintain a holiday schedule has in practice always proven to be very useful.*
>
> *It ensures that everybody knows of everyone when he or she may or may not be present. This allows for project employees to coordinate their work and to not come across any surprises. Estimating the number of available resources will also improve and can, where necessary, provide for suitable backup. Planning issues can be noticed prematurely and you can align your schedule upon it.*

9.4 Resource management

No project without resources

Resource management is highly organisation dependent because you need to follow the processes and procedures of the Human Resources (HR) department. You are also dependent on available tooling and maturity level of the organisation's project resource management.

Step 1 Who does what?
With resource management in a project you go by the Product Breakdown Structure (PBS) or Work Breakdown Structure (WBS) that has been set up. See the previous chapter about planning.
In here it states which products the project will deliver and when. In order to deliver these products you need your project employees. You determine per product which resource roles and competences you need.
These roles are often already described within an organisation and are usually available via intranet sites or HR. If the roles are not available, you can describe them yourself.
Which knowledge and skills do you need and what is the required level (junior, mid or senior or the required number of years of experience within the role)? Sometimes it can also be agreed with a client that a particular role must have a qualification. For example, a team leader should at least be qualified for project method x and speak English.

Step 2 How many resources are required?
Once you know what roles and associated knowledge you need, you go and acquire the required capacity. How many hours do you need to implement a certain product (or task) and you compare this to the time you have available for this purpose. For example, in the schedule it states that a product should be ready in 1 week. However, to make the product you require 80 hours of a resource. Assuming a 40-hour workweek, you will then need 2 FTE (Full Time Equivalent) in order to finish the product in time. Note: if they still have holiday or have become sick, you will need more resources or more time! Never plan resources for 100%, 80% is more realistic.

Step 3 What do resources cost?
You now know what kind of roles you are looking for, what the person should be able to do and how many people you need. These roles will come with a certain budget. Depending on the organisation there are 2 moments when budget information is available:
1. Before you go and look for the right person.
   This is possible when the organisation has determined that there is a specific hourly rate for a certain role (or if it is agreed that way with the supplier of the resources). The client or the organisation in which you run the project can have framework agreements with suppliers in which fixed

9.4 Resource management

rates have been agreed upon. For example an SQL-programmer costs 120,- Euro an hour, regardless of who the person is.
2. Only when the right person has been found.
   When there is no standard hourly rate per role agreed upon, you are dependent on the person that you have found. You will then only know after you have found the person, what the hourly rate will be. Often you can only deploy the person when the budget has been agreed. And as a result, the person might have already been hired by somebody else before you got the chance to deploy him/her. To prevent this, an estimate is made of the hourly rate and you will have to work it out later with the person during the negotiations.

Step 4 How do you acquire the right resources?
Now you can start looking for the right people for the roles. To do this you place a vacancy. How to place a vacancy and which criteria they must meet depends on the organisation. In any event, you can look at 3 areas:
1. Are there people within the project who could fill this role? This is usually preferred because they have already been working on the project and in the organisation. Besides, you already know what they are capable of.
2. If people are not available within the project, you will then go and look within the organisation. Internal people are generally cheaper to hire than external people. The danger is though, that people are being deployed who do not quite fit the profile. As a result, training time on the project will increase, which can in turn affect your schedule.
3. If no one is available internally, then you can look for external people. Disadvantage is that they usually have no knowledge of the organisation. On the other hand, a fresh pair of eyes and a certain expertise that is now missing, can also give an acceleration.

When you know which part of the organisation will deliver the people, you will go with the responsible manager and see whether the person is available and an intake interview will be conducted with this person.

> The withdrawing of internal employees from the (line) organisation can sometimes be very difficult. For this purpose, agreements must be made with the relevant line managers and no formal contracts drawn up. Managing these employees is an art in itself, as these are often experts who are very important in their own field. For that reason they often draw their own plan. Commitment of these employees is even more important than with externally hired employees.

9.4 Resource management

Step 5 What does a project employee need?
When everything is organised in terms of agreements and contracts, the employee can start. There are still a few matters to deal with:
- Access to the work location.
- (Virtual) workplace.
- Rights to applications and systems in which the employee must be able to work (network, intranet, SharePoint, mailbox, servers, applications etc.).
- Possibly screening. This is for example required in banks and government agencies so as to protect themselves from taking any high risk profile employees on board.
- It is sometimes asked to sign a confidentiality form; it can also be that such a clause has been taken up in a framework agreement with a company, so that, by definition, the employee of this supplier meets the requirements and therefore does not need to sign a declaration of confidentiality.

In addition, the employee can be added to mail groups for, for example, a newsletter of project focused groups. Or you select the e-mail addresses from the resource register.

On and Offboarding:
A new team member needs to be invited to project meetings. And given access to several buildings and systems. It is also useful to equip him/her with various general and technical facts. Be mindful of matters like how to print, how to book a meeting room and how to reach the PMO. Ditto for offboarding in which you keep track of whether all rights, accesses, registers and overviews have been updated. On and offboarding can also be executed by somebody with administrative responsibilities. If this person is available.

Template: example of onboarding project employees

Name : <name> Action required:	Comment	Ready (date or tick)
Work contract signed		
Account requested	Requested ddmm <account name> received	
Requested access to x		
Handed over welcome package		
Etc.		

9.4 Resource management

Step 6 What else can we collect about all resources?
Create a database (or Excel) of all the people you have hired. Mention all important details like: name, personnel number, phone number, e-mail address, (mobile) phone number, hourly rate, role in project, utilisation percentage, duration of deployment contract, perhaps licence plate for reserving car spots, in which team the person is in.

Template: Resources hire register

Name (and role)	Contact details	Deployed in plot/team	Supplier	Hourly rate	Utilisation %	Start date contract	End date contract

It is also useful to create a separate holiday schedule. In which it states who is when on holiday and who will replace the person in question. This can be organised by simply asking the employees when they will be on holiday. However, the continuity of the project is of importance. Also ask who their replacements are and whether there is no overlap with other critical people.
To get a visual overview, you can create a calendar schedule. This is also useful to have of the steering committee members, internal and external suppliers and other key stakeholders.

Step 7 Understanding the capacity schedule
As mentioned, resource management is going by the Product Breakdown Structure (PBS) schedule or Work Breakdown Structure (WBS) schedule. This schedule can now be customised with a capacity schedule. Employees can now be linked to the product or task in the schedule. In there it is mentioned when he or she is working on it (start and end date) and for how many hours. There are tools and applications available where the employable hours of the employees can be recorded. Also the holidays of the employees can be entered in this. The tool then calculates whether sufficient hours have been scheduled for the realisation of the product or task. Of course you can also use the tool when it is still unknown which employees will be available. In that case a dummy role will be entered.

Obviously you do this work in consultation with the project manager. You need to agree in advance which matters will be dealt with by the project manager (for example the intake interviews) and which by the PMO employee (for example the first selection).

9.4 Resource management

At the end of every project phase a recourse review needs to take place by the project manager and the pop-up PMO. The current project resources will be evaluated here asking whether they still add sufficient value. Have we got too many resources or rather too few?

Things only have the value that we give them.
Molière

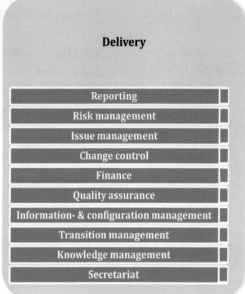

9.5 Benefit management

Objective:
Facilitate that the business case and benefits that a project must achieve are and remain clear.

> Nice, a pop-up shop, but why do they do it? What is the goal? The PMO employee raises critical questions, asks for the business case and aids in the formulation of indicators to measure whether the benefits will be realised.
>
> The pop-up shop does not have to make a profit. Breaking even is good enough. The organisation wants to use the shop as a sort of training location for new pop-up shop employees. The turnover of the resources will be high and the level of experience lower than normal. Something to take into account in the resource management process; it will require a lot of extra time.

Which stakeholders are involved in this service?
- Client / owner / senior responsible owner (SRO).
- Senior managers.
- Business change manager.

What can the PMO do at setup?
- Help plan and assess the benefits to be achieved with the project end results.
- Help identify and quantify the benefits (or review them).
- Draw up benefits realisation plan (together with the project manager).
- Make sure that the benefits are being added to the project documentation (like a business case) and that these are being updated at every phase.
- Facilitate that it is clear how, when and by whom the benefits are being measured.
- Help setting up a benefits review plan (the benefits realisation plan).
- A plan for measuring the benefits after project closure.
- Assist in setting up the business case.
- Verify that also the negative benefits are being identified.
- Facilitate that stakeholders and project manager agree with the identified benefits (and a benefits realisation plan).
- Create benefit profiles (a description per benefit).
- Create a benefits folder (sort of matrix of project products versus benefits).
- Prioritise benefits (which are most important to monitor); this not only prevents an overload of work, it also helps take decisions faster later on in the project.
- Execute baseline measurement.

9.5 Benefit management

Controlled progress
- Safeguard that benefit reviews are being conducted.
- Monitor the benefits by means of monitoring the measures or actions.
- Advise the project manager on changes that may affect the business case.
- Facilitate and advise the project manager in determining the benefits of the project.
- Execute benefit reviews (compare desired benefits with (already) realised benefits) and take action in accordance to the review results.
- Collect information for the purpose of the report about benefits realisation.
- Monitor the benefits realisation plan. This will go further for a programme than for a project.

Techniques and tools to be used
- Business model canvas.
- Managing Successful Programs (MSP) items:
    - Benefits Management Strategy
    - Benefits Realisation Plan
    - Benefits Map
    - Benefit Profiles
    - Benefits database or spreadsheet.
- Radar diagram to report about benefits.
- Workshop for identifying programme benefits and creating a benefits model.

Risks
If this service is not being set up properly, then one runs the following risks:
- Project loses sight of what objective it serves (except the project outcome).
- The initial business case is being lost out of sight.
- Measuring benefits at the end of the programme has as disadvantage that it cannot be adjusted in the meantime.
- Wasting time and money because the added value does not (anymore) meet the initial expectations.
- Too much focus on project product instead of on improving the organisational performance.
- Delay in decision making and the change management process, because every issue can lead to discussion.
- Lack of support and conflict of interests between the stakeholders.

9.5 Benefit management

> *I sometimes come across project managers who are of the opinion that benefit management is only for programmes or the responsibility of the business. Here is still a lot of missionary work to do. Fortunately, there is an increasing awareness that also within a project, besides delivering the project results and products, an eye must be kept and remained on the to be realised benefits (added value of the project result).*

9.5 Benefit management

Repeat the "Why" question regularly

The business case and associated to be realised benefits answer the "Why" question of a project.

A business case is more than a piece of paper[8] and is about much more than just financial goals. It is about the reason why the organisation is doing the project, in other words the motivation, the reasoning, the accountability or the justification of the investment. The business case is the relationship between the project and the interests or objectives of the organisation or the business strategy.
This will eventually be drawn up in a document that describes the business case, explains and substantiates, based on, among others, consideration of costs, benefits and risks.

The benefits can be defined as 'all that is positive as outcome of the project'. Besides euros there are matters like reputations, user satisfaction, transparency towards customers, safety etc. Also determine which benefit is the most important (prioritising of the benefits).

At the start, for example during a kick-off session, it is good to give a moment's thought to the "why question" with the entire team and with the steering committee. The best thing is to (have) translate(d) this into a "one-liner". That gives direction and motivation to the project team. During the following phases is it useful to regularly keep repeating the "Why do we do this project" question. This is sometimes being lost sight of in the news of today and also at times by the project manager and specialists.

Realise that the definition of a successful project is "if it delivers what was agreed upon at the beginning, according to scope, schedule and within budget".
Why then can clients still be unsatisfied afterwards?
In the current world, developments follow each other up more rapidly and grab onto each other, as well economically, socially, politically as technologically. Therefore new demands are constantly being set. It has become increasingly common that we, no matter how careful we prepare a plan, have to move the milestones during the duration of a project. Nowadays project management is shooting at moving targets and adjustment is permanently necessary. The change process plays an increasingly important role.

Involve beneficiary in the defining and realising of benefit management, this greatly helps strengthen the platform.

---

[8] Waarom doen we dit eigenlijk? - De businesscase als succesfactor voor projecten, Michiel van der Molen (2010) ("Why do we actually do this? – The business case as success factor for projects" Only available in Dutch)

9.5 Benefit management

The Why question also helps to strengthen the focus and leadership and to secure the implementation of the project result.

> The Dutch national museum has been renovated. The scope of the project has been adjusted many times, the project cost 3 times as much as was initially estimated and the museum has been closed for a few years longer than originally planned. Yet everyone is so enthusiastic about the result and it is called a hugely successful project. Why? Because during the project they had a constant focus on what the objective should be of the new national museum and subsequently guided towards it.

If you tell the truth, you don't have to remember anything.
Mark Twain

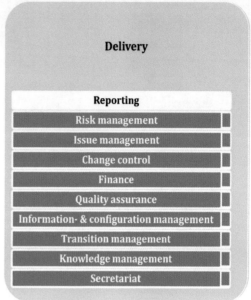

10. BUILDING BLOCKS: DELIVERY

10.1 Reporting

Objective:
To have and to give insight in the status, progress and expectations of the project by collecting and analysing data and information. Process and aggregate these into management reports.

> The project manager has asked the PMO employee to bi-weekly collect all information on progress, issues, risks and financial status. The setup of the pop-up shop is on schedule, however, there are some risks that appear to require extra attention, like the lack of clarity about the temporary connection of electricity and water. The project manager is very pleased with these reports, it provides a mechanism to just check a few details with the team members and then, after a few minor adjustments, send it on to the client.

Which stakeholders are involved in this service?
- Client.
- Steering committee.
- Controller.

What can the PMO do at setup?
- Draw format/template for reports and communicate this to the team.
- Set up and implement the report process.
- Determine the different target groups. For example an internal steering committee report and a separate one for the client.
- Agree on which reports are being done, when and who does them (PMO employee, project manager or a combination).
- Design the consistency and timing between the reports and monitor them.

Controlled progress
- Collect data and process into report(s).
- Advise the project manager on any points of interest or on decisions to be made.

Techniques and tools to be used
- Balanced scorecard.
- Definition of traffic lights (red, amber, green, when do you use which one).

10.1 Reporting

Risks
If this service is not being set up properly, then one runs the following risks:
- Steering committee cannot steer or steers on incorrect information and assumptions.
- Incorrect project expectations of stakeholders.
- Project manager is insufficiently in control and cannot manage his project well.
- Management receives different numbers at the same time, because the basis of the reports has not been consolidated at the same time.

> Everyone often has their own perception of when a status gets a certain traffic light colour. Within a project this has not always been agreed upon beforehand with the client/steering committee.
>
> This is one of my most used:
> 1. **Red:** need help from a higher layer of management (portfolio manager, steering committee, business manager etc.).
> 2. **Amber:** something is not going right, delay or other serious point of attention. Everything is under control, actions have been plotted. It is still dry, however, we have intensified the monitoring of the dykes.
> 3. **Green:** There are no issues or the issues are small enough to mean no risk.

10.1 Reporting

The right of reporting

Reporting is an important means of communication and steering, especially for the project manager himself. And also for the client/steering committee and for the team members.

The advantages of reporting are:
- Through the report you can make sure that steering can happen.
- It is a form of expectation management.
- It is a useful communication tool.
- It forces a moment of reflection (looking back and ahead). The report is a learning tool for the person who compiles it. It provides insight into your own functioning (successes and failures).
- You hold control of your schedule and points of action.

In short, it is the tool to be in control of the project and to be able to manage the project.

Some pitfalls in reporting are:
- Excessive use of project jargon and acronyms.
- How the project thinks about itself does not match with how the rest of the organisation sees and experiences the project.
- Conclusions are drawn from the report by misinterpretation of the information. It is therefore necessary that a report can be orally (or if need be, by phone) exemplified.
- Have the tendency to cover itself by the reports. Especially in case of problems and tensions the project manager will not enter into dialogue, and rather justifies setbacks through the report.
- The project manager knowingly leaves information out of the report, so as not to cause any agitation. This happens in situations whereby the steering committee is trying to control the project manager's job too much or even acts like a sort of extra work group.
- From the organisation a template and frequency are being imposed, which does correspond to the wishes of the client.
- An imposed template cannot always simply be re-used for other target groups. For example, you would like to re-use an extensive internal report for a less extensive external report.
- Focus is only on time and money, whilst a project includes more than just that.
- People who need to supply information are too late with this. Chasing it up costs (precious) time.
- A report is per definition always behind the reality, which goes faster. The report is a kind of time photo. Prevent steering on outdated data. Put very clearly the date and possible time in the report. Ensure that input is being processed quickly and that the report reaches the interested party as quickly as possible.

10.1 Reporting

The biggest pitfall is the perception that reporting is mandatory. In a report you not only look back but you also give a projection towards the end goal: are you, with the knowledge of that moment, capable of reaching your results.

On what can be reported?
Whether there is or is not a mandatory template, it is always useful to establish with the client and steering committee what will be reported on.
Every project and every organisation is different, yet you see several matters return in a lot of reports. Possible project Key Performance Indicators (KPIs) on which can be reported are:
- Retrospective (particulars previous period).
- Foresight (special activities and to be reached milestones).
- Course of schedule (possible mentioning of products ready).
- Periodic budget utilisation & prognosis.
- Update risks and actions.
- Issues and deviations.
- Changes and their status.
- And other in the project plan agreed parameters.

Multiple reports (for example internal and external), how can you be smart about it?
Certain situations require different reports for different stakeholder groups. Think of situations of fixed price projects for a client. The client wants progress information and so does your own company (internal client). A part of the content is often the same and a part will be different or absent. For example, with a fixed price project the client does not need to know the full utilisation of the budget, however the internal client does.
Tip: think carefully ahead about the whether or not mandatory templates and information. See how you can cleverly combine this. Create one comprehensive basic report and take out the information (or cut and paste smartly) that is not relevant to certain stakeholder groups.
Ensure that PMO is the SPOR (Single Point of Reporting).

Periodic and / or special reports
The NCB3 of IPMA writes about reporting:
When the project manager and/or the project team are very experienced, it may be adequate and acceptable for the stakeholders to report 'by exception'. This means that a report will only appear when something important needs to be reported, instead of monitoring through regular status or progress reports.

Special reports are, for example: phase end report, deviation report, project end report or learning points report.

10.1 Reporting

Whether or not to outsource to a PMO employee
Creating reports is a valuable tool to manage the project. All the things that need to be done to manage the project provide information to use in the report.
Seen from that point of view, a project manager should do the control of the report himself. Nevertheless, the pursuing and obtaining of the input for the report can be done by the PMO employee. The PMO employee will draw up a draft report. Ultimately, the project manager himself will benefit the most when he goes through the draft report and completes it.

> *Coffee tip from current practice:*
> *When a project manager creates the report himself and the following is being noticed, it is time to go for a coffee and ask a few questions.*
>
> *Report is very long (many words). The theory behind this is whether the project manager really knows what is going on in the project. Because when the project manager needs a lot of words to indicate what is going on, does he or she really know what is happening? In short: report should be specific and to the point.*
>
> *In the report everything is mentioned precisely three times on the schedule. And there is nothing special to report. In short, at a quarter of the project he has realised 25%, halfway he is 50% ready and at ¾ of the project he is at 75%. That cannot be true; the project manager has automated the progress report. You do not create a schedule to do things 100% that way. Due to the schedule you are able to, along the way, take better and faster decisions to respond to unexpected events.*
>
> *Mark*

*If the highest aim of a captain were to preserve his ship,
he would keep it in port forever.*
T. van Aquino

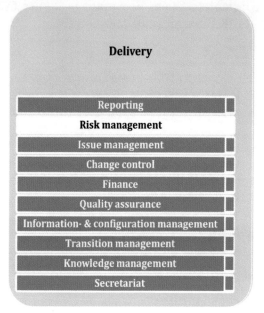

10.2 Risk management

Objective:
Consciously and explicitly deal with threats and opportunities, so that decision-making can be accelerated, the project will become more manageable, one can act more proactively and therefore prevent issues.
Risk management is actually mainly about whether one accepts the risks or rather wants to limit them with (against) risk responses.

> The PMO employee has facilitated a valuable risk assessment workshop. There have been many potential risks, opportunities and risk responses inventoried. One of the biggest risks and external dependency is the temporary connection to electricity and water. As a risk response, an emergency generator is kept on stand-by.
> The PMO employee updates the states of the risks on a weekly basis, checks if measures have been taken and looks whether new potential risks loom up.

Which stakeholders are involved in this service?
- Risk manager or risk management department or risk coordinator.
- Suppliers.
- Steering committee.
- Client.
- Audit and control department.

What can the PMO do at setup?
- Establish risk management strategy.
- Request company guidelines (risk management policy, codes of conduct, manual risk management processes, risk management strategies).
- Define standards and processes for project risk management and communicate these within the project team.
- Create project risk management tools and templates.
- Set up risk register.
- Collect risks (initial inventory, possibly already mentioned in contract or tender).
- Organise workshop to make an inventory of risks.
- Advise the project manager on risk management methodologies.

Controlled progress
- Maintaining risk register.
- Monitoring and pursuing of actions and measures.
- Documenting/directing/assigning of control measures.
- Maintaining of discipline and daily routine concerning execution of the control measures.

10.2 Risk management

- The regularly/periodically monitoring whether there is documentation demonstrating that risk responses have been executed effectively.
- Facilitating and advising the project manager in the managing of risks.
- Checking whether every risk has an owner and risk responses have been defined.
- Ensuring that communication is taking place with stakeholders that may be affected by risks or risk responses.
- Evaluating of executed risk responses and updating risk register.

Techniques and tools to be used
- List of risk categories as a tool for brainstorming like COPAFILTH (Commerce, Organisation structure, Personnel, Administration, Financial, ICT, Legal, Technology, Housing) possibly supplemented with Environment and Security.
- M_O_R (Management of Risk) of Axelos.
- Pre-mortem examination[9] (from the Gamestorming book).
- Project Risk Analysis and Management (PRAM).
- RASCI diagram (who is Responsible, Accountable, Supportive, Consulted and Informed).
- Risk matrix (Summary Risk Profile).
- RISMAN (originated from the Dutch Department of Waterways and Public Works and then further developed by a group of six organisations).
- Herringbone or Ishikawa diagram (cause and effect diagram).
- Probability tree.
- Workshop/brainstorming.

Risks
If this service is not being set up properly, then one runs the following risks:
- Inefficient use of resources (unnecessary work to correct the same mistake again).
- One loses out on opportunities.
- One is busy putting fires out.
- Many surprises and therefore extra costs.
- Dissatisfied stakeholders.

> *Many project managers have difficulty with this process because it pushes them into the role of bad news bearer. The focus is, despite the theory, on threats and less on opportunities.*
> *My experience is that project managers are happy when the PMO employee takes this process largely out of their hands.*

---

[9] Gamestorming: A Playbook for Innovators, Rulebreakers, and Changemakers, Dave Gray, Sunni Brown and James Macanufo

10.2 Risk management

When you can identify a risk, you can also mitigate it

The definition of a risk is "an uncertain event with impact on your objectives". By consciously addressing the setup of this process, the chance of success to reach your objective increases.

Issue and risk are closely related and are often mixed up. Of a risk you do not know for certain whether it is going to happen. An issue is a fact (something that has taken place).

A risk that comes true will then be managed as an issue. In addition, every issue can entail new risks.

Why not include risks and issues in one register?
Issues are more urgent than risks. Something has happened and usually requires immediate action.
The transfer of information from one register to another increases the effectiveness of the management processes.
There are other metadata being recorded with an issue or risk. With an issue you are not talking anymore about an increased chance (probability) or expected value. The PMO employee can regularly check whether there are no issues in the risk register.

Besides threats, opportunities (chances, possibilities) also fall under uncertain events. Opportunities are usually recorded under a different tab of the register. You want to maximise them instead of minimise (mitigate) like with threads.

All risks are registered in a central register per project and or programme, whereby at least the following details need to be registered per risk:
- Unique characteristic (serial number).
- Characteristics like name submitter, submit date.
- Description of the risk (cause, event, effect on the objective).
- Probability (chance) and impact (high, medium, low).
- Expected value (= impact * probability percentage).
- Risk responses (actions).
- Risk owner (is responsible for ensuring that the risk is being managed as well as possible and all selected responses are being taken).

Possibly added to it:
- Risk category.
- Cause of risk (what is the driver that could cause the risk).
- Secondary risks (characteristic of new risk to be recorded as a result of a risk response).
- Risk status (active or closed).
- Risk response category.
- Risk response status.
- Risk response action holder.

10.2 Risk management

Example risk register:

ID	Description	Opportunity	Impact	Identification date	Expected value	Risk response	Status	Risk owner

Risk response categories for threats can for example be: accepting, mitigating (softening), reducing, sharing or excluding. For probabilities they are for example: accepting, expanding, exploring, sharing or leaving.

Be grateful for whoever comes to report a risk! The task of the PMO employee is also to stimulate that behaviour.

What else can the PMO employee do:
- Check whether a correct formulation of the description of the risk has taken place.
- Are cause, event and effect clear.
- Make an assessment (or have made): probability and impact.
- Make an assessment (or have made) of proximity. At what moment can the risk occur?
- Ensure that the risk owner has been appointed and that he/she knows about it.
- Help conceptualise risk responses (for example send round the risk requesting input). Note that every risk response can also bring along new risks. Now we have come up with risk responses. Which ones are we really going to implement?
- Help name categories and check that a risk has been linked to a category. When there are many risks in a particular category, it may be useful to deploy a specialist.
- Help calculate the EMV (Expected Monetary Value). This is the sum of the weighted effects. EMV also says something about Risk Appetite, that is where it should start; compare with risk capacity.

Ensure that a risk budget is being allocated. Which budget do you need to manage a risk? Which budget is needed when the risk manifests itself.

The initial inventory of risk can be organised through a workshop. See also chapter 11 "Along with everyone: the organising of a workshop". Based on the stakeholder analysis you know who to invite for this. It is of importance to avoid socially desirable answers during this session. Someone who monitors the process and does not interfere with the content can facilitate this (for example a PMO employee).

10.2 Risk management

After initial analysis the risk management process will continue. Think of a new phase, unexpected changes, re-scheduling, deviations.

> **Three tips for risk planning:**
> 1. Start on time: Risks can be easiest managed at the start of a project and mitigating risk responses can then be taken.
> 2. Involve various stakeholders: The more people with different backgrounds are involved, the greater the probability of correct and full identification of risks (e.g. sales, legal, HR, finance, IT etc.).
> 3. Regular reconsiderations and re-evaluations: A risk register is not a snapshot; risks are dynamic and can change from week to week.

> The risk that risk management is insufficiently carried out often occurs with the type of project manager who is involved in the content and too "emotionally" connected to the realisation of the project result.
> The risk tolerance increases in those situations.

> *A "Conspiracy of optimism[10]" (over optimism) culture I have encountered in a lot of projects. We like to say that we have got things well sorted, until it is too late. This phenomenon particularly appears to be in environments where politically correct behaviour can be found in combination with commercial and competitive pressure. And where short term personal rewards take place.*

---

[10] Second order of project management, Michael Cavanagh

Step one of solving a problem is acknowledging that you have a problem.
Raffiek Torreman

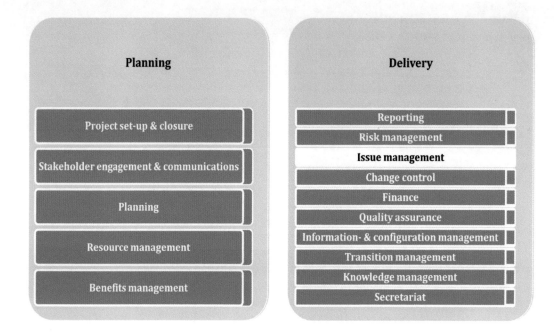

10.3 Issue management

Objective:
Every potential problem must be identified and efficiently dealt with as early as possible.

> The construction of such a pop-up brings a lot of questions and problems along. Who takes care of the champagne at the opening? The ordered floor carpet is too small and the size of the light fittings is still unknown.
> The PMO employee records all these issues in an overview and pursues the sequence.
> After a few days it is clear that a caterer has been booked for the opening that also takes care of the champagne. That particular issue is updated in the register and switched to dealt with.

Which stakeholders are involved in this service?
- External suppliers.

What can the PMO do at setup?
- Define issue management standards, issue process or strategy and tooling.
- Create issue management tools and templates.
- Create an issue register.
- Inform project team members on the work method concerning issue management.

Controlled progress
- Consolidate project issues in the issue register.
- Create status reports for issues (for example number of open and in certain periods closed issues, number of issues in a particular category).
- Monitor and report on issues.
- Disclose issues to the right person.
- Determine impact of project team and client and possibly escalate issues.
- Advise on issue solutions.
- Transfer the outstanding issues to line or management organisation at the end of the project (often in the form of residual points).

Techniques and tools to be used
- Issue database.
- Scoring and prioritising mechanism. For example MoSoCoW: Must have, Should have, Could have, Will not have.

10.3 Issue management

Risks
If this service is not being set up properly, then one runs the following risks:
- Not properly working product deliveries.
- Nothing is being done about risks that have become visible.
- There is no insight and direction on existing issues, because of which nobody does anything or multiple people are trying to solve the same issue.

> The PMO employee is usually not close enough to the project execution to identify the project issues himself. This is primarily the responsibility of the project managers and team members. It is the responsibility of the PMO employee to (have) record(ed) the risks and issues that affect the project in a central register, to bring these to the attention of the right people and to monitor that they are being resolved.

10.3 Issue management

The issue management process is a major artery of the project

PRINCE2 distinguishes the following types of project Issues:
- Proposed changes.
- Deviations of the specifications.
- Other problems or concerns.

Issues and risks have a strong relationship, because at the moment that a risk becomes manifest, it leads to an issue. Issues may therefore not come as a surprise, they have been predicted, if all has gone well, during the risk management process. Despite the relationship, risks and issues are being managed in different ways. Issues contain much more than established risks. In the PRINCE2 definition (project level) every question or problem that occurs and cannot be resolved immediately is an issue (also change requests).

Figure 10.1 Connection between Risk and Issue

The PMO employee can usually not resolve the issues himself, he can encourage and monitor (manage) the entire process around it.
The owner of the issue is somebody within the project team responsible for ensuring that the issue is being resolved.
An issue register should be transparent and maintained centrally.
Through tooling it may be possible that issues are being registered by project employees themselves. These can also be taken from reports. Something standing on Amber or Red means that an issue is at the bottom of it and requires attention. Besides the issues from the status reports, it is important that the PMO employee himself is alert on information from other channels (mail exchanges, conversations, meetings).

10.3 Issue management

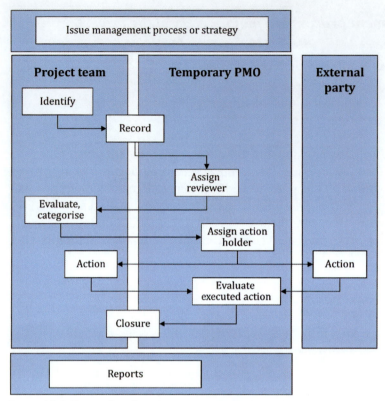

Figure10.2 Example of an issue management process

The other way around information on issues can be used in reports and for discussion and prioritising in meetings.
Ensure that according to a periodic (for example every week or during daily stand-up meetings) outstanding issues are being discussed.

It is of importance that the issues are being reported and especially that it is clear who the owner of the issue is and thus contributes to resolving the issue. Use mainly graphical reports like for example figure 10.3. Be clear about what is being expected of the resolution owners.

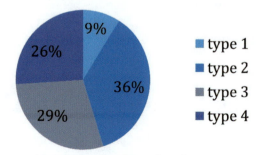

Figure 10.3 Example of graphical issue report

10.3 Issue management

Issues are being recorded in an issue register or log. The below example can, for instance, be supplemented with a column ready yes/no, priority indicator and when an issue needs to be externally dealt with.

Example issue register:

ID	Issue type	Description	Submitter	Date Submitted	Action holder or owner	Status update info	Closed on date
	<knowledge domain>						

Besides the issues, one can also report about the issue management process. For example monthly on how many issues there are in a given category. This can be useful towards management in order to demonstrate that issues are effectively being eliminated and as trend analysis to estimate when all of the issues can be resolved.

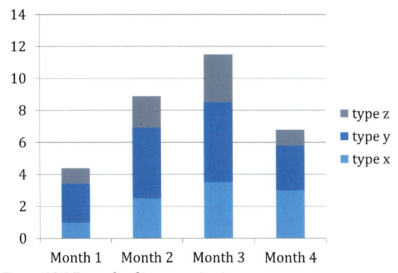

Figure 10.4 Example of issue monitoring

The issue management process can also be used in a test phase for a potentially separate findings register.

> Beforehand, it should be clearly decided what the definition is of an issue.

Nothing is permanent but change.

Heraclitus

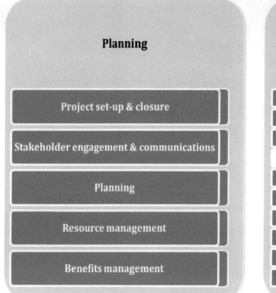
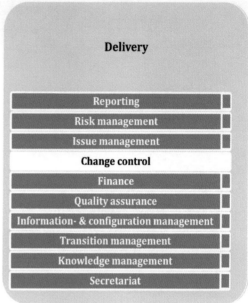

10.4 Change management

Objective:
Identifying, establishing and monitoring of changes. Facilitate at project CAB or change control board.

> **Unfortunately it appears that the pop-up shop will open one day later than planned, because the supply of some shelves got delayed. The PMO employee ensures that with help of the team all consequences are being inventoried and written down in a concept change proposal. The process that must now be followed further was already set up in accordance to the pop-up roadmap, so the client gave his approval on the change quite soon. After approval the resource hire schedule was adjusted. Shop personnel must arrive a day later and assembly personnel are hired one day longer. The PMO employee adjusts the budget accordingly.**

Which stakeholders are involved in this service?
- Client.
- Steering committee.
- Account manager.
- Controller.

What can the PMO do at setup?
- Define change process and template.
- Define possible report.
- Create scope management tools and templates.
- Register baseline scope information (in-control).

Controlled progress
- (Have) Analyse(d) the consequences of proposed changes for the project.
- Monitor and control the change management process (with every change). Taking action when process is not running well enough.
- Monitor project scope (including the consequences of decisions).
- Advise the project manager regarding the change in the scope.
- Check contract impact (is change included or not in the agreed contract agreements and what are the consequences?).
- Check resource management impact.
- Check the schedule (does it need adjusting?).
- Manage and after approval adjust the scope in the various documentation, systems and registers. Consider for example quality register, Product Breakdown Structure (PBS), schedule, risk register, test plans, product backlog (Scrum), financial system or sheet etc.
- Communicate the consequences of the change with stakeholders.
- Maintain change register including decisions.

10.4 Change management

Techniques and tools to be used
- Issue register.
- Scenario schedule.

Risks
If this service is not being set up properly, then one runs the following risks:
- Project is considered failed.
- Higher costs for execution of changes.
- Longer throughput time of project.
- Project does not deliver what organisation needs.
- An incorrect project administration and file.

10.4 Change management

Organise the change management process in advance to avoid project failure

Besides the fact that the project itself is a change of the "business as usual", changes can also occur within the project. We are then talking about a change of the predetermined scope (including requirements), budget, time or objective. So all cases where an existing agreement regarding the project between client and project, is being changed.

Changes within a project are inevitable. One should almost always, depending on the type of project, take into account a 30% to 50% extra project budget as a result of changes.

Possible causes of project changes are:
- The conduct of business gets a different need.
- The prioritising of projects has changed within the organisation.
- The organisation has changed (new products, location, departments, management, financial control etc.).
- Technological changes.
- New business partners or channels.
- Changing rules and regulations.
- Effects of other projects or programmes.
- Mistakes in the execution of the project (the least elegant unfortunately).

Projects that have not calculated and set this process up well are afterwards often labelled as a failed project. Well, and the PMO is also responsible for this.
The later a change is identified and treated, the higher the costs, risks and duration of the project.

Change versus issue
There is an overlap between an issue and a change. Issues can lead to changes. And vice versa a poorly executed change can consequently become an issue.
There is a separate process required for changes, because in many cases a change has consequences on financial, time, or quality aspects. Also the authorisations for approval of a change lie elsewhere in the project organisation than those of an issue. The changes must be approved by at least the steering committee.

You need to know a few matters in order to be able to set up the process:
- In what way are changes approved?
- Who approves the changes, who prepares them, who checks them, who registers them?
- Is a project CAB (Change Control Board) being set up and who is its chairman?
- Which template and procedure is being used?

10.4 Change management

- Which tolerances are there? Are there different levels of approval for changes of certain types or with certain costs?
- What are the connections between the other processes like issue and configuration management?
- How and where does the change register stand?
- How are approved changes communicated to the project team and other stakeholders?

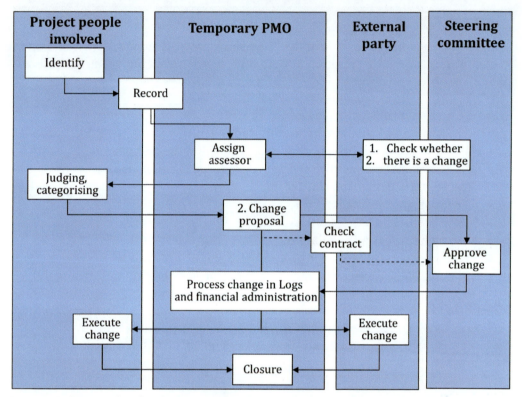

Figure 10.5 Example of a change management process

In terms of process, I have good experience with the so-called two-stage rocket.
Stage 1. The project manager or a team member first makes a brain dump. Does not perform extensive research. The project manager will coordinate with the client whether this is in fact a change.
Stage 2. When it becomes apparent that the change has purpose, time can be spent on further tests, research and balancing with others stakeholders and involved parties. This will prevent that a lot of time is being put into a change that might not be recognised.

10.4 Change management

Example change register:

Change ID	Domain	Short description	Request date	Sub-mitter	More or less work	Impact (money, time, schedule, quality)	Status	Date approved	Approved by
	<sub project or product>								

On occasion I have noticed that when a change comes under discussion, this can sometimes lead to tensions between client and contractor of the project. Especially with fixed price projects, where a change can lead to more or less work.
My experience is that a change is sometimes easier discussed with and accepted from a PMO employee who manages the change management process rather than from a project manager.
Adjust the process before there is a change.

At least 70% of the effort in this process must be spent on communication (beforehand, during and after approval of the change).

Ensure that approved changes are being announced to the entire project team and to the stakeholders.
Avoid using jargon in the communication.

Money is a fine servant, but a terrible master.

Unknown

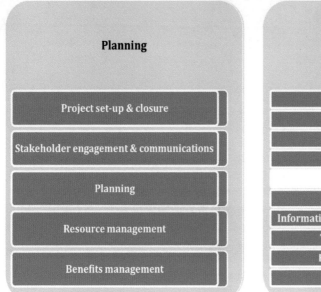
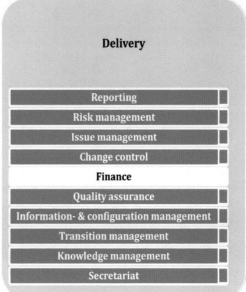

10.5 Finance

Objective:
Forecasting and monitoring of the project finances. Facilitate the process to be and stay financially in control.

> In consultation with the controller of the client it is being aligned how and when the utilisation of the budget is being maintained.
> The PMO employee will periodically give an update of the utilisation to the project manager. The change from the late delivery of the shelves and because of that the one day slow-down will cost one day extra assembly personnel. The budget will be raised with these extra approved costs, which were approved by the client.

Which stakeholders are involved in this service?
- Controller.
- Accountant.
- Financial administration.
- Billing department.

What can the PMO do at setup?
- Aligning of the financial project administration with the financial department.
- Creating of or determining a budget and resource prognosis template.
- Determining the necessary financial tools and implement these accordingly.
- Setting up financial project administration.
- Draw an overview of obligations, expenditures and budget.
- Aligning of financial status report template(s). This information can also be included in the project progress report.
- Framework of financial schedule and process to control budget utilisation.
- Draw mandating model.
- Mapping the process of handling invoices.
- Drawing format of the business case.
- Set up process and agreements around time writing.

Controlled progress
- Maintain financial schedule and tracking tools.
- Update budget as a result of changes.
- When a change occurs in the project, map the impact on the costs (give input to change).
- Maintain business case.
- Create a prognosis of cost trends and final costs.
- Give signal for billing upon achieved milestones.
- Draft up a report on financial prognosis (progress and dashboard).

10.5 Finance

- Sign off on timesheets.
- Check invoices and process these in the financial project administration.
- Check and approve hours in the time registration system.
- Link costs to resources.
- Process write-offs in the project costs.
- Map financial performance of the project.
- Signal and escalate when necessary to project manager.

Techniques and tools to be used
- Cost Benefit Analysis.
- Discounted cash flow technique.
- Earned Value Analysis (EVA).
- Net Present Value technique (NPV).

Except for EVA, these all can also be used when drawing the business case.

Risks
If this service is not being set up properly, then one runs the following risks:
- Understanding of project costs is missing.
- Costs of project cannot or are hard to predict.
- Project becomes more expensive than planned.
- Billing is done incorrectly, not or too late.
- Financial impact of changes is difficult to determine.

> Don't forget the PMO budget itself It is also part of the financial calculations and management. The performance of the PMO itself (including budget) needs to be tracked and reported on.

10.5 Finance

It is not about how much budget you have but about what you can do with it

At the start of the project it will be necessary that the project manager makes an estimate of how the predefined project budget will be spent. A large part of this budget often exists of man hours that will be spent. To keep control of these hours spent, the financial responsibility exists of an estimation on how and when to spend the required hours. This can be adopted in an hours & costs prognosis.
This estimation will, as the project progresses, have to be compared with the reality on the basis of the hours booked, the costs that are being made and percentage ready regarding products.
A useful methodology for this is Earned Value Analysis (EVA).
Working according to an Agile/Scrum method is also a way to, together with the client or product owner, by means of iterations constantly deliver a certain functionality (scope and value) for a certain budget.

Agreements are being confirmed with the project manager regarding the updating of the financial data. For example, a month to update the financial prognosis for an x amount of months. A printout of the hours booked can normally be made on a monthly basis so that the financial overview can be updated and can be compared with the predicted data. Necessity of this can be aligned between PMO and project manager. A good relationship should also be sought with a possible financial controller, who has the necessary data to, besides the timesheets, include the remaining costs in the calculation.

To arrive at a financial overview, the following steps will be taken:
- The hour prognosis is being included in a financial overview template.
- By linking the rates per hour of the employees to this, the costs will be calculated.
- At the end of a financial month, the actual hours (and rates) made will be included in the template.
- Additional expenses and/or orders are being added.

At this time, the forecasted costs can be compared with the actual costs made. Of these, reports will be compiled and communicated to the project manager.

Types of expenditure (variable and fixed costs):
- Location costs.
- Material costs.
- Personnel costs, through hours * hourly rate or invoices of hiring.
- Promotion, publicity and public relations (PR).
- System costs (licences).
- Organisational costs.
- Additional costs.
- Unforeseen costs.

10.5 Finance

With the financial administration it is useful to align what the billing triggers are and how this information is being passed on.

Changes are the only constant factors in a project
Before a change is being established, the PMO employee can be asked to deliver input on, among others, the financial aspects. The rate agreements are being consulted or quotes are being requested in order to give a detailed interpretation.

When a change is approved it must be processed in the financial systems. The budget is being updated, perhaps new codes are necessary in the financial system. The utilisation and reporting sheets need to be adjusted.
In case it is more work, an additional billing meeting will have to be scheduled on how and when these can be invoiced.

> Use a clear structure of project products with associated budgets and deployments. Let this be the basis of possible invoicing.

10.5 Finance

It can sometimes be quite an effort to get the actual budget above water.
An hourly rate calculation can be based on an average rate for a certain role. When it is an effort to find somebody for a role, you run the chance that the purchasing will be more expensive and that therefore the budget will need to be adjusted accordingly.
Especially in commercially offered projects there may be a difference between the costs calculated by the seller(s) and what the project manager thinks to make in costs.
A project manager should always make his or her own calculation whether or not helped by the PMO.

*Delivering quality costs money,
not delivering quality costs a fortune.
(Unknown)*

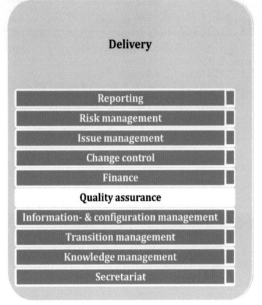

10.6 Quality assurance

Objective:
Ensure that agreements are being made about the quality of the project products and the project management processes and that these agreements are being followed up.

> There are some parts of the project of which have been determined beforehand that these have to be accepted formally. For example, the cash register system must meet a number of predetermined criteria and eventually be accepted by the accountant. All this "product" delivery information is being maintained by the PMO employee in a sort of register (logbook). Due to this, he/she can also see what remains to be done and what possibly has to be followed up.
> The PMO employee also notices that in the communication plan a number of other data is being used than in the project plan and has offered some suggestions for improvement.

Which stakeholders are involved in this service?
- Quality manager.
- Contact person for tracing the internal and external audit requirements (in case there is no quality manager).
- Supplier.
- Acceptors.

What can the PMO do at setup?
- Implement quality management processes and tools.
- Set up critical success factors.
- Check whether the project meets the compliance (law and jurisdiction).
- Determine and register project quality standards.
- Participate in establishing the project quality plan. In case the PMO employee fills the QA (Quality Assurance) or quality control role as a specialist, than he or she will set up the plan.
- Establish who will accept project products and according to which acceptance criteria. This can be done in a quality register.

Controlled progress
- Maintain the quality documents.
- Check quality monitoring checklists.
- Inform project members about guidelines and quality standards.
- Control and monitor the execution of project management processes.
- Take initiatives to improve project management processes.
- Signal and report deviations.

10.6 Quality assurance

- Execute audits on project products or direct them.
- Review management products and/or the coordination of it (quality control).
- Facilitate in audits by planning the meetings, providing the necessary documentation, attending the meetings, possibly establishing (part of) the audit and help communicate and implement recommendations from the audit.
- Execute the additional activities in the quality plan.
- Guidance of the acceptance tests and the evaluation of them.

Techniques and tools to be used
- Audits (in-depth research into the functioning and success potential of the project).
- Health checks (global check of the functioning of the project on the basis of predetermined criteria).
- International guideline for project management ISO 21500.
- ISO9126 quality criteria and other ISO norms.
- Quality register (or logbook).

Risks
If this service is not being set up properly, then one runs the following risks:
- Unsatisfied customer, client and team members.
- Schedule is exceeded due to unclear review, test and acceptance agreements.
- Fines for exceeding law and regulations.

10.6 Quality assurance

The first time that I was asked to review a project plan, I skimmed through it. What should I pay attention to? Meanwhile, I now have a short checklist for this.
- *Consistency with organisation and programme terms.*
- *Consistency of word usage.*
- *Spelling mistakes.*
- *Logical language usage.*
- *Uniformity concerning other documents (template).*
- *Usage of acronyms (explanation).*
- *A QA (Quality Assurance) paragraph in every PID.*
- *Have all project management processes been adequately described.*
- *Is there a risk analysis? How will it be maintained?*
- *How about tolerances? Are they SMART enough?*
- *Are the PMO tasks appointed?*
- *Consistency of the to be delivered (sub) products with other documents like the Product Breakdown Structure (PBS), project plan, quality plan.*

10.6 Quality assurance

Quality is as good as the weakest link

In regards to quality, who is responsible for what during the project?[11]
- The client is responsible for the ultimate use of the project result, thus for effectuating the assets as described in the business case. The client or a delegate has a seat in the steering committee.
- A representative of the users (senior user) is responsible for the quality of the user input in the project. And looks after the assessing of the requirements. The user input is also important during the development, the testing and of course the implementation. This representative sits in the steering committee.
- A representative of the supplier(s) is responsible for the quality of the delivered means and employees. And sits in the steering committee.
- The project manager is responsible for the quality of the project organisation, as well as for the project processes and the project result.
- In addition, every employee in the project is responsible for the quality of their own process and own result.

Optionally, a separate quality officer can be appointed. If he or she is allocated from the steering committee, one talks of project assurance or quality assurance. If the project manager delegates tasks, one talks of quality control. Quality control is a PMO function that the project manager can do himself or outsource. The tasks that are usually being delegated are the monitoring of processes and products and securing that effective measures are being taken.

Quality management can roughly be divided into two areas:
1. The project organisation.
2. The project products.

Figure 10.6 shows this schematically and will be further explained after this.

---

[11] Quality Assurance in projecten. Wiebe Zijlstra, ZBC kennisbank, 23 February 2011 http://zbc.nu/ ("Quality Assurance in projects" Only available in Dutch)

10.6 Quality assurance

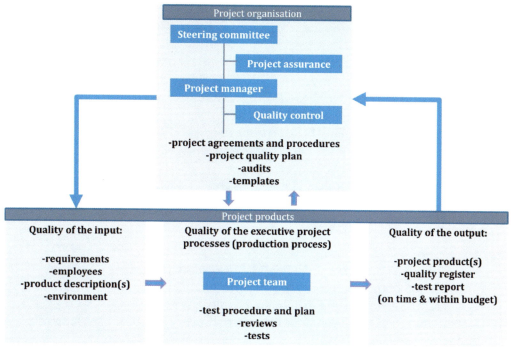

Figure 10.6 Coherence between the different quality aspects in a project

1. **Quality of project organisation (project management and processes):**

A good senior PMO employee mainly provides many qualitative advantages. This goes beyond the project support role like PRINCE2 describes. A project manager can leave part of managing the project organisation to him or her. This will go by means of clear agreements and agreed processes. A PMO employee often sees like no other where the weaknesses are in terms of project management.

The pop-up PMO can ensure the quality with an individual project by encouraging that the project and the processes at least comply with the following requirements:
- Connection to standards: is there adequate connection to standards and requirements of the environment/organisation.
- Quality procedure: is there a sufficiently clear description of the quality techniques to be used? Are working methods prescribed, guidelines mentioned and a description given of the required knowledge and skills to achieve the quality.
- Acceptance plan: which acceptance activities are included in the project plan? Are these activities sufficient to meet the required acceptance criteria? If desired, these activities may also be included in the project report as an assurance.

Also of importance is that the PMO employee is not afraid to escalate to the project manager when project stakeholders do not comply with the agreements. As a PMO employee it is useful to create and maintain your own file for that.

10.6 Quality assurance

Make notifications/escalations officially, make sure that your warnings have been well-documented.

2. Quality of project products:
Ten steps have been defined for products that are covered by quality control in order to guarantee the quality. The following should be covered by quality control in any case:
- The products that are being transferred as project result.
- The most important (sub) products of every end product.

In the quality register all products that are covered by formal quality control are listed. The register also contains the planned and actual dates of the steps for all products.

The 10 steps are:
1. Definition of the products (PBS: Product Breakdown Structure).
2. Identification of the acceptors for every product. This includes both end users as well as those who have a management role.
3. Documentation of the acceptance criteria that every acceptor uses for every product.
4. Establishing test plans that point out in detail which tests are to be performed and what the expected outcomes are of the tests and which deviations are still acceptable.
5. The building of the project products by sufficiently adequate personnel, whereby, if it has been mentioned in the test plan, "peer reviews" are being used for intermediate results.
6. Comparing of the product with the acceptance criteria independently of the builders (internal system test).
7. Recovery of found deviations and errors, then back to step 6.

N.B.: Steps 8-10 may not be applicable to all products, they are mainly intended for end products.
8. Comparing of the product with the acceptance criteria by the acceptors (acceptance test).
9. Recovery of found deviations and errors, then back to step 6 (not 8!).
10. Formal acceptance.

These 10 steps can be planned and also monitored so that, if necessary, action can be taken in time.

When projects run out of time, there is often a tendency to let go of the quality standards or follow them less accurately.

Substantive tests of project products take place in step 3, 4, 6, 8.
A PMO employee can monitor, establish and report on the progress at every step.

10.6 Quality assurance

Example quality register:

Product nr	Product name	Acceptance criteria	Test plan	Test or Review	Name acceptor	Plan acceptance date	Acceptance date
<from BPS and schedule>		Status where to be found?	Status where to be found? Or N/A	Status			When accepted?

Monitor the consistency between the products mentioned in the project product descriptions, the Product Breakdown Structure (PBS), the quality plan, the necessary capacity, the risks and the reporting on the status of products in the reports.

Make everything as simple as possible, but not simpler.
(Albert Einstein)

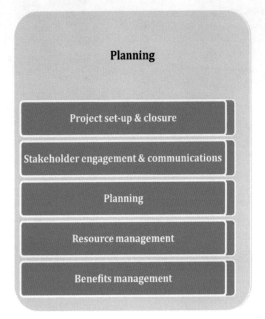
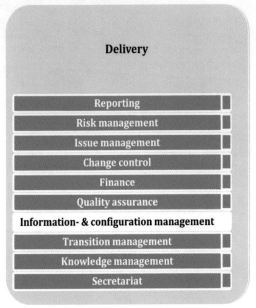

10.7 Information & configuration management

Objective:
Be able to execute coordination of and be accountable for reproducible, traceable project and management products of the project.
This process regulates agreements on:
1. Naming conventions of project documents.
2. Agreements on how to deal with project documents (in terms of storage, review procedure, approval procedure, version control).
3. Construction and maintenance of the project archive.

According to P3O this service is the most important to set up with a pop-up PMO.

> **Where is the latest version of the shop floor plan? What is the difference between internet connection and fiber? To prevent these kinds of questions, the PMO employee organises a sort of temporary mini library with access to all necessary information, for example documents. Just like in a real library, uniform agreements on usage of terms and what version number have to be made.**
>
> **The PMO employee appears to be a centipede, because having knowledge of archiving methodologies and systems is in this process very handy/practical.**

Which stakeholders are involved in this service?
- Functional and possibly technical controller of an information and/or document control system.
- Archivist where the company guidelines can be requested.
- Security officer.

What can the PMO do at setup?
- Set up a documentation or configuration management plan.
- Draw up version control agreements and cycle. In addition to documents also for project products such as software.
- Arrange naming conventions.
- Establishing and setting up document and information structure (establish index), of all sorts of information that may arise in the project (project products, decisions, contracts, changes, milestones achieved, actions etc.).
- Set up an electronic document and information environment.
- Make agreements on what is recorded, how it is available and to whom it is being made available. Make protocol agreements. For example, only documents that have been signed (with name and date) will be archived.
- Make agreements on form within the project and with the client: for example oral agreements are confirmed and recorded in writing (per e-mail).

10.7 Information & configuration management

Controlled progress
- Maintaining document structure.
- Maintaining the electronic document and information environment.
- Control the project documents and information. Ensure that the last official (possibly signed) versions have been saved.
- Identify possible issues in regards to project products.
- Execute configuration audits (check whether the project products that should be there, are actually there and with the same version number).
- Maintaining the document and information structure (index).
- Check whether information, documentation or parts that are to be delivered by a potential supplier, are actually there.
- Record decisions, changes, additions and milestones in a uniform and logical way.
- Archiving of agreed documentation (also make backups).
- Make confirmed documentation available.
- Classify documents.

Techniques and tools to be used
- Document management system.
- Information site (intranet, internet).

Risks
If this service is not being set up properly, then one runs the following risks:
- Discussions on what the latest correct version is of a document.
- When having a weak position in the event of legal action or disputes, likelihood of claims.
- Project team loses a lot of time with searching for information.
- Incorrect versions of documents are being used (e.g. outdated versions).
- Information that should not (yet) be made public, is undesirably being leaked.
- Old already corrected mistakes from earlier software releases (or iterations) are resurfacing.

A good project file has the following characteristics:
Accessible: traceable and logically arranged, stored in one place. Accessible to those who work with it and not accessible to unauthorised people.
Complete: All decisions, plans, agreements, changes etc. should be systematically present. Especially when political or financial accountability is important.
Current: During the project, the file must always be properly updated. In case of handover/transfer, audit or legal necessity.

10.7 Information & configuration management

Does your project file look like the cutlery drawer at home?

What does your cutlery drawer, in your kitchen, look like at home?
Neatly organised? Small knives separated from the big knives? Do you not envy the left cutlery drawer?

Or have you got everything mixed up together, like in the right cutlery drawer?
As a result:
1. lose a lot of time searching;
2. miss because it is not there;
3. use the wrong knife because you could not find the right one quickly
etc.

A project file is the same.
A well-structured file, with only the latest approved versions built up logically, can prevent a lot of project misery. And in case of disputes, the file must be legally watertight.
Decisions, changes, additions and milestones with contractual and financial consequences have to be updated and recorded in an unambiguous way in the project file.
Logical folder names, sub folders, consistent document naming and version control are a must. But what is logical?

The following approach forces you to think logically about the structuring of all information and configuration items within a project.
1. WHAT will you save? What types of information?
2. WHY and for what purpose per target group?
3. WHERE will you place which information and with what structure?
4. HOW will you record it?

1. WHAT will you save? What types of information?
Distinguish between project management and project result products. However, also the information before the start of the project, like possible quotes, calculations or contracts.

10.7 Information & configuration management

2. **WHY and for what purpose?**
   - Is it about the ability to consult information?
   - Is it about archiving and file formation to withstand an audit successfully (be audit proof)?
   - Is it about document collaboration?

This can differ per target group. A particular version of a plan should merely be insightful for one group, however someone else does want to be able to change and update it.

3. **WHERE will you place which information and with what structure?**
Think in advance about what you save, in which system or in which folder.
May or should certain information be placed on the internet or intranet site?
Is there a SharePoint system, central drive, document management system or project management tool where information can be saved or in which can be worked together on project products?

A directory structure that I often use and that is methodology and phase independent:

Level 1	Level 2	Level 3	Docs	Explanation
Management				
	Change control			Register, procedure, template
		Change nr 1		Per change a folder with versions, final signed change, correspondence, related documents
		Change nr 2		
	Contract documents			For reference
	Issue management			Register, procedure, template, correspondence
	Finance			Baseline, full utilisation information, procedural agreements
	Quality management or QA			Quality plans, register, procedures
	Consult	Consult <name A>	YYMMDD	Per consultation a folder with calendar, concept and final notes, action & decision register, attached documents. E-mails as proof of mailing
			YYMMDD	
		Consult <name B>	YYMMDD	

10.7 Information & configuration management

Level 1	Level 2	Level 3	Docs	Explanation
			YYMMDD	
	Schedules			
	Reports			*Template, procedures*
		YYMMDD		Per report moment/group a file with input and output documents
		YYMMDD		
	Risk management			Register, correspondence, procedure
		Meeting x		Material in preparation and output
	Resources			Register with commitment contracts information
		Name A		Per project employee commitment contracts, correspondence/e-mails regarding commitment, CV
		Name B		
	Stakeholder management	Stakeholder information		Telephone/e-mail list, stakeholder folders, analysis etc.
		Newsletters		
Project products				Folder structure based on the PBS
	Category/team x	Work documents		Are in development, intermediate versions
		Final approved documents with proof		E-mail/scan or signed document/signed acceptance declaration
	Category/team x	Work documents		
		Final approved documents with proof		

4. **HOW will you record documents?**

Ensure that in the index the latest approved version has been documented. This can be through a separate quality register or through a comprehensive Product Breakdown Structure (PBS) that will be further completed. When you work in a folder structure like Microsoft, you can save older versions in a folder named archive, so that in the main folder you always have the latest version visible. There

10.7 Information & configuration management

are also electronic tools available for working on documents in a team, document management and version control. For example, SharePoint and Projectplace. Record decisions and agreements with a financial or legal significance, like test results, acceptances and (technical) changes, clearly and legally signed.

Ensure that a decision that has been taken in a steering committee is being noted and confirmed during the next steering committee meeting. In the minutes you put a reference to the minutes of the previous time and mention that these are hereby approved.

> **TIP:**
> You can merge the Product Breakdown Structure (PBS) and the quality register and include a link in this register to the location of the latest official version of concerning document.

Version numbering is also a topic on which you make agreements in advance.

> **Example version control guidelines:**
> 0.1 Start.
> 0.2
> 0.3 First internal review.
> 0.4
> 0.5
> 0.6 Version for quality assurance control by PMO or QA department.
> 0.7 Possible second version for quality assurance control by PMO or QA department.
> 0.8 Version for the acceptor for approval.
> 0.9 Possible modified version in response to comments.
> 1.0 Final version with approval of acceptor (possibly with signature).

Agreements should also be made on naming conventions.

> **Example naming convention:**
> Project name (document type, yyyymmdd) version number (possibly initials during reviews).
>
> For example:
> Pop-up Shop (PID, 20130219) v2.1
> or
> Pop-up Shop (main points report, 201300315) v1.0 MM

Make sure that everyone abides by the agreed rules concerning recording and filing. Do you notice that this is not being done, you can then escalate to the project manager.

10.7 Information & configuration management

To properly compile a watertight project file you need experience and time. You can capture a part in the agreed project governance. However, in the end it comes down to consistently, accurately and orderly maintaining the file.

Audits

One of the reasons for correctly maintaining a project archive is being able to account for the proper execution of the project should an audit occur.

In order to meet up to an internal or possible external (from the client or a regulator) audit, it is necessary to know at which points this will be performed. This can be sorted out and the points made known to all the members of the team at the start of the project. It can therefore be necessary to employ heavier quality demands or to execute a heavier form of configuration management.

An audit is not always announced at the start of a project. It may very well be that your project is being nominated for an audit during the course of the project. It is therefore important that you always have everything in order.

Security

Check which guidelines there are from the organisation. Certain information in a project should never be placed in a generally accessible environment and may only be accessible for a limited number of people. Think for example of:

- Contract information of hired employees with rates and private addresses (Data Protection Act).
- Financial information of the project (you do not want hired employees of possible competitive companies to be able to access this information).

Consider with each type of information whether it is convenient that everyone can read it. Even though everyone may sign a confidentiality agreement: prevention is better than cure.

A good end is the entire work.
The court jester

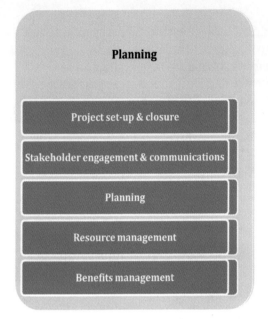
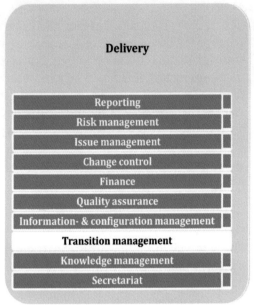

10.8 Transition management

Objective:
Ensure that the project results and products are properly and timely transferred to the existing organisation (operation) or client.

> Soon the pop-up shop will be ready, the building crew is leaving and then other personnel can take over. What instructions are useful for these people? Shall we already give them a tour?
> The proposed shop personnel may want to start thinking about the layout of the kitchen, what is being used for the coffee and lunch break? Basically this is of course the task of the entire project team and the project manager to think about. In practice these appear too busy with having the pop-up shop go live before the set deadline. Since the PMO employee is a centipede, has organisation sensitivity and is less being sucked into the hectic of the project itself, he or she can very well help facilitate this transfer.

Which stakeholders are involved in this service?
- Line managers.
- Administrators.
- End users.
- Change Advisory Board of the line organisation.
- Transition manager in the line organisation.
- Service manager.
- Functional manager.
- Facility services.

What can the PMO do at setup?
- List the products and services to be transferred, for example transfer and revision documentation, courses, manuals. These products are named in the Product Breakdown Structure (PBS).
- Request a management control checklist or (management) acceptance criteria.
- Align (and have agreed of) mode of granting closure (discharge) or draw up closing statement.
- Organise process and template for acceptation of project products.

10.8 Transition management

Controlled progress
- Assist business change managers in transitions.
- Transfer responsibilities from the contractor to the client.
- Compile transfer and revision documentation.
- (Have) Organise(d) training for those who will use the project results.
- Handover operational documents.
- Record outstanding points of attention or residual points.
- Ensure that project gets official closure (discharge). Include this closure in the project file.

Techniques and tools to be used
- ASL.
- BiSL.
- ITIL.
- Service management.

Risks
If this service is not being set up properly, then one runs the following risks:
- Project is being thrown at management.
- Management is too late and not aware enough of what is coming at them.
- Residual points are not sufficiently transparent.
- Resistance with management to take control of project results.
- Projects slumber on.
- Possible claims.

10.8 Transition management

> *I have several times been in projects where, due to highly squeezed contracts, the focus was entirely on delivering only the agreed end results as soon as possible for the lowest cost.*
>
> *The receiving organisation was totally unprepared to receive the end product of the project, resulting in a lot of complaints and questions from managers, administrators and users.*
>
> *I understand the project manager though, because he will be judged and served in such a way that they will blindfold him. The client of a project needs to understand what they ask and buy and have a good understanding of what else needs to be arranged and organised.*
>
> *This must therefore be called a high risk at the start of the project!*

10.8 Transition management

Operation successful, patient deceased

Each project has a delivery to two parties, being the party(s) that will use the project result and the party that will manage it. Management can also be distributed over multiple parties, the direction and responsibility is frequently seen lying with one party.

In some organisations there are special transition managers. This manager is responsible for a soft landing in the managing party. This is particularly a common role in the ICT.
A transition manager ensures knowledge securing with the managers, organising the financial charge and structuring the existing management tooling to be able to react adequately to messages and requests from end users. These are aspects on which the project manager often spends little attention.

If there is no transition manager available in an organisation, then one should be appointed. This can sometimes also be the project manager himself. The project manager is always responsible for the delivery to both the (end) users and the managing party.

The project should, although this may not be in the scope of the assignment, always have eye for quality, information and communication towards the managing organisation. When this does not happen sufficiently, you know in advance that problems will arise in the operational phase. Especially in trajectories where you as external party are responsible for the execution of the realisation.
Avoid the phenomenon "Operation successful, patient deceased". In other words, the project result is delivered, but the organisation has major problems with it afterwards.

A proper transfer of the project result starts already during the project. Create baseline and maintain at the future users, already during the project activities or even before. Think of providing the expected requirements and acceptance criteria by the users or a representative thereof.

Components of the project deliverables can be introduced in a Change Advisory Board (CAB) of the managing organisation.

I notice in trainings that the term "changes" can sometimes be confusing. A project or programme is a change within the organisation (company), changes can also occur within the project when the agreements made beforehand change, such as scope, time, money, quality. In addition, a project can have a change as a result of the managed "assets" (configuration items) by the line organisation. I have summarised all these types of changes in figure 10.7.

10.8 Transition management

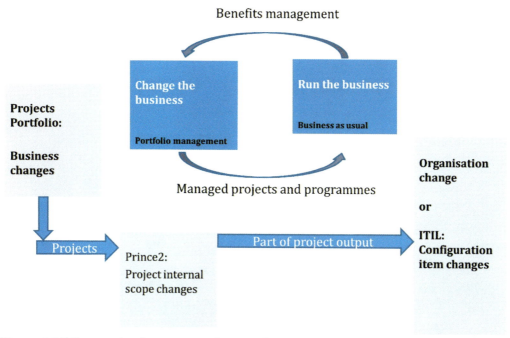

Figure 10.7 Connection between projects and ongoing management

There is only one thing more painful than learning from experience and that is not learning from experience.

Archibald McLeish

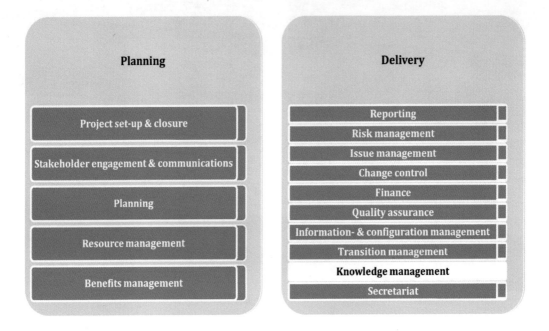

10.9 Knowledge management

Objective:
Bring, share and retrieve from lessons learned on other projects.

> Last year there was also a pop-up shop project. Unfortunately there is nobody present from the old team. The PMO employee retrieves a lot of information on that previous shop by making a few phone calls and shares this with the new team. Because of this, for example the evacuation plan for the fire-brigade does not need to be fully recreated.
> After delivery of the pop-up shop, the PMO employee organises a so-called "lessons learned" session in which all do's and don'ts are being collected for future projects. What went well? What would you do differently next time. Besides for a future project, this is especially important for the self-learning abilities of the employees involved. You learn, so you grow.

Which stakeholders are involved in this service?
- Other project managers.
- Everyone who has ever been part of a project or contributed to it.
- Manager/administrator lessons learned database.
- Steering committee.
- Corporate board.
- Client of the project.

What can the PMO do at setup?
- Look up sources of lessons learned. This can be in the form of documents or databases and in the form of names of people whom can be contacted.
- Collect lessons learned of previous projects and share with the project team.
- Set up lessons learned register or project logbook (sort of blog).
- Set up a FAQ register (questions and answers concerning the project) for team members and/or end users.
- Set up facts and/or welcome document for new project members. It is especially useful with long term projects where there is a high turnover of resources to have a document or webpage with a summary of the project (objective, organisation and facility services).
- Create insight in which team needs knowledge and which project employee can deliver what kind of knowledge and expertise.
- Map the vulnerability of the project team in terms of knowledge.

10.9 Knowledge management

Controlled progress
- Maintaining FAQ overview (questions and answers concerning the project) for team members and/or end users.
- Add to lessons learned register of project with lessons learned following sessions, issues and deviations, information from reports.
- Update a possible central lessons learned register.
- Organise and facilitate lessons learned session(s).
- Consult previous lessons learned registers from previous projects.
- Facilitate in solving problems.
- Take care of iteration reviews.
- Collect the project velocity profiles.

What can the PMO do at closing the project?
- Make lessons learned register available to the organisation.
- Evaluate effectiveness of tools.
- Initiate the adaptation of project management processes and tools in consequence of lessons learned.
- Facilitate a project evaluation session.
- Evaluate work packages. Was the estimation correct or what would you do differently next time.
- Provide work packages with documenting evaluation in a work packages library. What are the actual hours made and have any particulars happened when realising the work package?

Techniques and tools to be used
- After Action Review.
- Agile or scrum retrospectives (evaluation after an iteration, so interim and regular).
- Best practice database or other type of repository.
- Forum.
- Knowledge management system.
- Learning matrix[12].
- Matrix employability of the employee. Map employability (knowledge and competences) employees.
- Root Cause Analysis (RCA).
- Workshop.

---

[12] Gamestorming: A Playbook for Innovators, Rulebreakers, and Changemakers, Dave Gray, Sunni Brown and James Macanufo

10.9 Knowledge management

Risks
If this service is not being set up properly, then one runs the following risks:
- Project members can make the same mistakes as other colleagues.
- The wheel is being reinvented, causing unnecessary costs.
- Maturity level of the project organisation remains low.
- You lack insight in what knowledge is required for a certain project product, problem or phase.

> Knowledge management within project management can be distinguished in:
> - Process knowledge (project structure, methodology, tasks and schedule),
> - domain knowledge (like construction, ICT, industry or government),
> - institutional knowledge (history, values and how things work in the organisation) and
> - cultural knowledge (cultures of different blood groups in the project team, like IT architects, managers and web designers).

10.9 Knowledge management

Acquire, monitor and secure knowledge before, during and after a project

Projects that invest in securing knowledge (with the turnover of project members), individual learning experiences, organising active knowledge sharing and utilising best practices, prove to be more successful than projects which have no or hardly an eye for this. (According to research by Karlsen & Gottschalk, 2004; Lierni & Ribière, 2008; Hong et al., 2008; Anantatmula & Kanungo, 2008).

Knowledge management consists of retrieving and bringing. And gain timely insight into what knowledge you need.
Before the start of the project you want to bring the right knowledge together to start the project. Knowledge is needed from similar previous projects, from the environment, the to be developed product or service, the (user) market, and so on. For that, you consult earlier lessons learned or colleagues.

During the project you want to be smart about the knowledge of the project members. Try to avoid loss of knowledge. Make sure you have mapped out who possesses what knowledge. Create channels for knowledge transfer. Develop a collective team memory. Create an atmosphere where learning is being encouraged.

Is someone leaving before the end of the project (planned or not), arrange for an exit interview. This can yield a wealth of information.
After completion of the project you want to secure your knowledge for the line organisation and for possible future projects. This is usually referred to as lessons learned.

Options to collect lessons learned:
- Open survey.
- Targeted product evaluation.
- Targeted process evaluation.
- Circle meeting or group discussion.
- Assessment interview.
- Right-wrong method.
- Retrospective.

If this is done in a group, it is important to:
- Align objective of the assessment.
- Predefine the points to assess.
- Regularly summarise.
- Stay on the case, as the probability of straying is very high.
- Give everyone a chance to speak and do not talk through each other.
- Draw conclusions.
- Create a report and share this with the attendees.

10.9 Knowledge management

Potential evaluation topics:
- Functioning as project team.
- Project management.
- Techniques and tools used.
- Schedules, work packages, cost and time calculations.
- Has the desired project outcome been realised.
- Are the benefits as expected.
- How is the actual Return on Investment compared to the planned.
- What went wrong and what went right.
- What would you do the same next time and what not.

Template: lessons learned register

ID	Category of learning point	Description	Registered by	Prio (rity)	Action description	Action holder

To avoid that lessons learned disappear in a "grey" archive, you need to ensure that something is done with it. That is why it turns out to be necessary in practice to link action holders to lessons learned. Apparently you want to have something happen or not next time. Who will organise, communicate and secure that in the organisation?

> It is not just about the retrieving of knowledge with the familiar "lessons learned" sessions, it is particularly about the managing and applying of knowledge.

No grand idea was ever born in a conference, but a lot of foolish ideas have died there.
F. Scott Fitzgerald

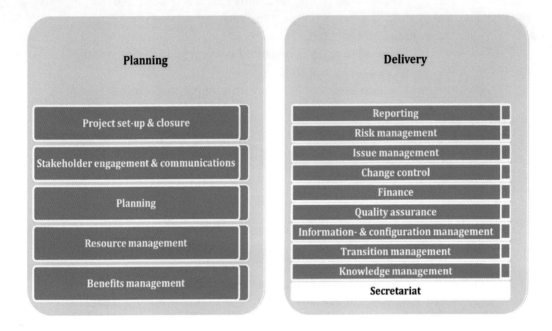

10.10 Secretariat

Objective:
Relieving the project organisation with regards to organising and making reports of agreements, meetings and gatherings. Organise facility services.

> It takes a lot of patience and perseverance of the PMO employee to align all the calendars of everyone in order to get that kick-off session and steering committees organised.
> By being allowed to report on the most important discussions, the PMO employee remains well-updated on what is going on.

Which stakeholders are involved in this service?
- Secretaries (of for example the steering committee members).
- Administrative assistants.

What can the PMO do at setup?
- Find out who the secretaries are of the steering committee members.
- Sort out process and templates for calendars and minutes.
- Find out how facilities like rooms, catering and office supplies can be organised.
- Create register to record the communication from or to the client or other parties.

Controlled progress
- Establish steering committee calendar, organise any additional guests (for example, a specialist who comes to explain something).
- Collect documents on behalf of the steering committee (previous minutes, the to be discussed parts).
- Organise facility services for steering committee or special meetings (kick-off, soapbox session, etc.).
- Maintain register of communication to or from the client or other parties.
- Write steering committee minutes.
- Manage agenda (calendar) for project team.

10.10 Secretariat

Techniques and tools to be used
- Consultation framework[13].
- Clock agenda[14].
- Listen, summarise, question (LSQ).
- Steno.

Risks
If this service is not being set up properly, then one runs the following risks:
- Poor or no record of decisions.
- Poor preparation of the steering committee, which will cost time of those present.
- Team members who independently of one another spend time organising facility services and office supplies.

> Ask yourself the question whether extensive reports have added value. An action and decision register will suffice in many organisations. I see too often that minutes are standardly approved time and time again, whereby I wonder whether they are actually being read at all. You can probably save yourself a lot of work.

---

[13] Het groot verbeterboek, Neil Webers, Lucas van Engelen & Thom Luijben ("The great improvement book" Only available in Dutch)
[14] Gamestorming: A Playbook for Innovators, Rulebreakers, and Changemakers, Dave Gray, Sunni Brown and James Macanufo

10.10 Secretariat

Whether or not secretariat activities?

A secretariat is usually essential for a large project with many meetings at strategic level. It relieves the project manager of a lot of administrative organising work and rigmarole.

By secretariat various activities are understood, like:
- Prepare and report for steering committee meetings.
- Plan meetings, organise training and user acceptance tests, write or maintain overviews.
- Maintain loan administration of for example laptops or other items.
- Organise facility services.
- Organise access and authorisations.
- Organise IT tools and support.

A secretary also facilitates in the convenient sharing of other useful information like organograms, maintaining contact lists, templates and is a source of information regarding these topics.

The in the previous paragraphs mentioned processes and services (building blocks) are often difficult to combine with secretarial work. These often cost a lot of time, whereby the focus on securing the project results and quality of the project management processes might come in a fix.

The advice is to, if possible, pass the secretarial tasks on to somebody whose profession it is. This can be a specialised PMO employee in this field.

I once treated myself to a pen which records the conversation whilst you write. By later clicking on the written text, you can hear exactly what was said at that time. A very handy tool named "Livescribe".

10.10 Secretariat

A hate-love affair with the steering committee

As a beginning PMO employee or at a pop-up PMO where you are the only PMO employee, you often cannot avoid to at least facilitate the steering committee.
It is very interesting and instructive to sit in on such a meeting, because you hear and see a lot. However, the writing of the minutes itself I personally always found rather an awful job.
The writing of minutes should not be underestimated. It is a time consuming and specialised task. Calculate for 1 hour of taking down minutes, an average of 2 hours elaboration time.

- A regular meeting (you have had time to prepare yourself, participants use a comprehensible language, you can hear everyone, chairman leads the meeting tightly and logically):
  1 hour meeting = 1 hour writing minutes.
- A tough meeting (you are well-prepared, however you do not always understand what people are talking about, meeting is at times messy or you cannot hear everyone as well):
  1 hour meeting = 2 hours elaborating.
- A heavy meeting (you could not really prepare for it, people use difficult language, meeting is chaotic or participants cannot always be heard):
  1 hour meeting = 3 hours writing minutes.

Minutes serve a number of objectives:
- Report of the conversation, also for non-attendees.
- Reminder to all participants.
- Evidence of made agreements.
- The basis for a new meeting or actions.
- Archive of documentation.

The role of the secretary is to orderly and relevantly summarise in a document what has been said during the meeting. You do not take part of the meeting yourself. You stay neutral and can of course subtly correct on following the agenda and monitoring of the meeting time.

During the steering committee meeting, there are a number of moments where you as a PMO employee can certainly interrupt, if you find that this is not done by the participants themselves.
- Ask (if the chairman does not do this him/herself) whether the minutes of the previous time can be approved. Mention adjustments to the previous minutes in the minutes of the current meeting. Only then will the previous minutes be legal and audit proof.
- Check the content of an action point. Have I correctly understood that xxx is being done? Make sure it is clear what, by whom, when is being done.
- Ask who will take the action, when this has not been mentioned clearly. With conference calls (meeting over the phone) it can be that you do not recognise a voice, do not hesitate to ask.

10.10 Secretariat

- Ask the chairman to conclude decisions or make the first move yourself.
- Ask when the next meeting will take place.
- Feel free to ask questions when jargon or acronyms are being used that you do not yet know. Also avoid the TLAs (Three Letter Acronym) without explanation in your minutes.

Finally, a number of tips for elaborating the minutes:
- Mention who was and was not present and the date of the meeting.
- Mention the documents and meeting documents that were, besides the minutes, introduced and discussed. Per document you record: title, date and version number, format (Word, Excel, PowerPoint presentation etc.).
- Distinguish between the various agenda items.
- Stay neutral and objective in your text. Do not add information when this has not been mentioned during the meeting. It can sometimes be useful to still add information that has become known after the meeting. This can be done by adding a note, in a different format, from the minutes secretary. For example:
  [Note from the secretary: it is now known that ...].
- Properly record decisions in a table after or with the minutes, adding the date and serial number.
- Write your minutes as soon as possible after the meeting. It is professional, what has been said will largely still be in your memory and people can take action faster in response to the report.
- Check for language and spelling mistakes.
- Have the minutes read by the chairman or project manager before sending them.
- An option is to send round the first version of the minutes with "draft" mentioned in the text and file name. After approval and any adjustments in the following meeting, the original minutes will be circulated with the word "final".

Keeping a decision register can be useful when there are multiple committees in which decisions are being made.

Template: decision register

Nr	Date	Decision description	Committee
SG001	27-20xx		Steering committee
SG002			

10.10 Secretariat

A good start is half the work. Read the previous minutes thoroughly. Study the agenda and the possible extra meeting documents.
Prepare the meeting with the chairman. Which decisions have to be taken? What is the objective of the meeting?

11. ALONG WITH EVERYONE: THE ORGANISING OF A WORKSHOP

If I Tell you, you will forget
If I Show you, you will remember
If I Involve you, you will understand
Benjamin Franklin

A task of a PMO employee is the organising and supervising (facilitating) of project meetings.
Project meetings often take place before and during the project execution. For participants an active and involved form is a workshop. Project outcomes are in practice found to improve by using workshops within projects. Workshops create:
- More speed in your project.
- Higher quality, by using collective knowledge, especially with complex topics.
- More support and understanding.
- Greater efficiency.
- Improved working relationships.
- Joint ownership of outcomes.
- Lowered risk of scope deviations.

What kind of workshop could you for example think of in a project?
- Kick-off session with steering committee members.
- Kick-off session with project team.
- Risk assessment workshop.
- Stakeholder identification and communication planning.
- Planning session.
- Process design.
- Business requirement session.
- Create communication plan workshop.
- Sessions to create support with stakeholders.
- Lessons Learned meeting.

Note that a workshop is really a workshop when all participants are equal to one another (no ranks and classes) and through an open dialogue actively participate in the outcome. This does not mean that there are no ranks or classes, you do not just wipe them away, make sure that ranks and classes do not play a dominant or disruptive role.

11. ALONG WITH EVERYONE: THE ORGANISING OF A WORKSHOP

The use of well-considered methods, so that everyone has an equal chance to contribute, is for example a way to ensure that difference in ranks and classes is not or works less disruptive.
An effective project workshop is well-prepared, professionally managed and delivers clear results, and clear follow-up and agreements about it, how to monitor the follow-up and possibly communicate about it.

Should a project manager do this himself?
Project meetings are in practice often prepared and led by the project manager. It is sometimes useful to outsource this to an independent facilitator, like the PMO employee.
What should you pay attention to when you are the one to manage a workshop?
- Ensure equal input of all participants. Manage group dynamics.
- Control that people listen carefully to one another.
- Monitor time during the session.
- You need to be able to stay objective and neutral regarding the content.
- Stay patient. Do not intervene when the participants struggle to reach the outcome of the workshop. The struggle is often just as important as the outcome.
- Built a bridge between technical and non-technical information. Ask what certain acronyms or jargon mean. Chances are that there are more participants who do not know this, however, are afraid to say so.

It has a number of advantages to ask a more independent facilitator for interactive meetings.
- The facilitator is impartial, which may be handy when there are conflicting interests or opinions.
- Participants get (instinctively) more opportunity for initiative. The hierarchy is becoming more neutral because the facilitator does not belong to one of the hierarchical components. The project manager can actively participate as far as content goes.

The facilitating of a workshop can be done by a PMO employee, providing he/she is trained and experienced.

How do you take on preparing and facilitating a workshop?
The Dutch book "Hartelijk Gefaciliteerd" written by Jeroen Blijsie and Annet Noordik delves into the designing and facilitating of workshops within organisations. Jeroen and Annet also train people in this. The below five-step plan explains the five phases from which a good meeting has been set up. You can request the checklist of activities corresponding to this five-step plan for free via the website www.hartelijkgefaciliteerd.nl (in Dutch). As a facilitator, you are the director and that already starts beforehand at the preparation. A thorough preparation is essential for the success of the workshop and the achievement of the objectives.

11. ALONG WITH EVERYONE: THE ORGANISING OF A WORKSHOP

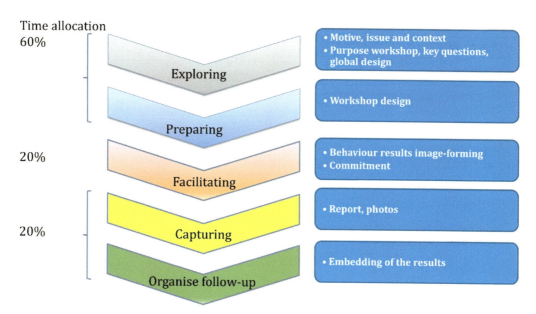

Figure 11.1 Five-step plan for organising a workshop

For the first two phases a template has been added at the end of this chapter.

What in practice creates a lot of positive energy and commitment is the use of a visual approach. Not by giving a presentation, however, by visibly capturing everything that has been said or been produced in front of the entire group. This can be done on flipcharts, workshop boards or via a laptop and a projector. The visualising of topics, which means that participants or the facilitator work with pictures during a meeting, also works very well. After all, a picture sometimes says more than a thousand words.

The capturing of the results, visibly for everybody, and working with pictures in it, instead of only with words, has certain benefits:
- Visual capturing confirms directly that somebody has been heard and can serve as a check whether somebody has been understood.
- It stimulates both the left and the right side of the brain. Most people typically use only one part of their brain, the left hemisphere. Logical, linear thinking, analytical ability and intellectual functions are located in this cerebral hemisphere. Our upbringing and education are largely based on this. The right hemisphere contains our intuition and emotions which are not being stimulated in our western culture. It gives us the ability to make creative connections and see through spatial processes which allows us to take the right decisions.
People who use both sides of the brain are more creative, smarter, more enthusiastic and more passionate, feel better and can better cope with work pressure and generally have a higher work discipline.

11. ALONG WITH EVERYONE: THE ORGANISING OF A WORKSHOP

- The black/white thinking is being prevented. More is often possible with pictures than with words.
- It gives more possibilities to talk directly about how someone sees or understands something.
- Working with pictures enhances the imagination of people.
- Existing or desired patterns become visible sooner.

Techniques and tools to be used

There are many different creative visual methods. The book "Visual meetings" by David Sibbet, gives a good overview. They can be divided into 3 types of tools:
- Visual communication. By, for example, using different colour pens on flipcharts or brown papers on the wall.
- Post-its, image cards, mind mapping software or other tools that divide information into small chunks.
- Idea mapping in graphical templates and worksheets, like business model canvas, flow chart, graphs or Gantt chart.

Further methods (for example):
- Group graphics® keyboard (The Grove Consultants International)[15].
- Introductory methods[17].
- Metaplan method, brown-paper or post-up[16 and 17].
- Storyboarding[17].

Finally, do not forget to record and secure the outcomes of the workshop. You can take photos and then paste them into PowerPoint. The advantage of this is that it is recognisable for the participants, that it really is a mutual result and not a translation from a secretary.

Also think ahead of time about what is, in practice, going to happen to the outcomes of a meeting. Who will communicate which information and in what way? Who will take on which follow-up actions, and especially: who will monitor the following up of the action? Will there be a follow-up meeting or will the workshop outcomes be continued in regular meetings?

---

[15] Visual meetings, David Sibbet
[16] Hartelijk Gefaciliteerd, Jeroen Blijsie and Annet Noordik ("Happy Facilitated" Only available in Dutch)
[17] Gamestorming: A Playbook for Innovators, Rulebreakers, and Changemakers, Dave Gray, Sunni Brown and James Macanufo

11. ALONG WITH EVERYONE: THE ORGANISING OF A WORKSHOP

> I was once at a kick-off of a merger and reorganisation of my company. Hundreds of people in a big conference hall in the Netherlands. The beat of drums rippled through the hall. We had to clap along and filled the hall with energy. A speech by the highest boss and one by one the executives came on stage under great applause. A new strategy was presented. They also wanted to know from us, what we could contribute to this. Everyone was allowed to write on a card with optionally your name written on it. Everyone began to write furiously. The cards were returned. Wow, I was allowed to think along and was going to be heard! I could not wait for a message to take action. After the drinks, everyone left in one big traffic jam from the parking lot, home. Full of expectations and enthusiasm…
>
> We NEVER heard of it again. No idea what happened to all our ideas on the cards. Big grey archive? Confidence in such management and your own organisation goes rapidly downhill then.

11.1 Project kick-off with steering committee members

The summit is, as a PMO employee, to be able to lead a project kick-off workshop with the involved project manager(s), team leaders, PMO team, suppliers, steering committee members and the client. This workshop can partly take the place of step 3 (gather information) and 5-8 (design project processes, PMO organisation, tools and techniques, information and communication) of the 10 steps in chapter 6.

For the design of the workshop you can also browse through the topics in the book "Project management for project executives". You can add to these by going into more detail on the previously mentioned project building blocks (processes). By standing still at each relevant process, you touch all the topics mentioned in the book in a somewhat more structured way.

Firstly, something about the book "Project management for project executives"
Besides an explanation on how a steering committee works and how a project executive can manage a project manager, in the 133 pages are also mentioned 4 very necessary tips called "Principles".
Principle 1: Share the business case.
Principle 2: Organise ownership.
Principle 3: Focus on deliverables.
Principle 4: Empower the project manager.
The project executive is the one who manages the project manager (often a line manager).

In the workshop you can have the participants think about the 4 principles, wrapped up in questions like:

1. Share the business case
It is good to, during the project kick-off, stand still together with the project team at the question behind the question/assignment, the "why question". Understand why the client wants this. What is the business case? "Why are you doing this project?", "When will you be satisfied?", "When is the project a success?".
Make sure you get answers that go beyond the execution of the project. The so-called dot on the horizon. The benefits to be. Or in other words, the question behind the question.
In case there is no project name yet, you can have them come up with it in the workshop. Formulate a slogan for the project that radiates the purpose. Also a metaphor can serve as a tool here.

11.1 Project kick-off with steering committee members

2. Organise ownership

The project team and the project manager are for success often dependent of other (groups of) people. Create support is a familiar cry. In particular the project executive and the steering committee members play a crucial role in this. You can assist by providing insight and structure.

Monitor and stimulate that the steering committee is not only connected with the goal of the project, however also feels an individual responsibility to deliver a specific contribution to this goal.

It is important to clarify to the steering committee members what their role, tasks, and responsibilities are. Has everyone got the necessary authorisations or mandate to take decisions? This is not always clear, with as a consequence no timely or incorrect decision making.

Ensure that you get answers to questions like "Who are the stakeholders?", "Who is going to sit on the steering committee?", "How do we engage as many project stakeholders in as early a stage as possible?".

"Who is responsible for the communication and creates the communication plan?" This plan states who, what and when communicates and through which medium.

3: Focus on deliverables

Make sure that it becomes clear which products the project will deliver. Many projects have the tendency to think in activities. Thinking and managing of products has a number of advantages[18]:

- It creates more transparency.
- It provides a SMART definition of the work to be carried out, expressed in (sub) products.
- It provides clearly described work packages that can be delegated or outsourced.
- It makes it possible to make more accurate estimations about the work content, the costs and the required resources.
- It makes better management, control and reporting of the project possible.
- It ensures that risks can be better identified and mitigated.
- The breakdown fits a top-down specification process seamlessly.

Working on a PBS based schedule has two other important advantages: for the project executive (client) it is important to know when he gets certain (sub) products delivered and the contractor can link invoicing moments to the delivery moments of the (sub) products.

---

[18] Product-Based Planning, Adri Platjes in SCHIP&WERF de ZEE April 2007 (in Dutch)

11.1 Project kick-off with steering committee members

Project executive and steering committee like to steer towards milestones. Therefore, ensure that you also get an answer to questions like:
- What are the milestones of the project?
- What are the go/no go moments?
- Which clearly identifiable stages can we apply in this project?
- Will the project budget also be progressively made available, if so, at what moments?

4: Empower the project manager
A steering committee in principal only meets at deviations/exceptions. To know what a deviation is, you first need to clearly define the project on the aspects of scope, quality, money, time, risks and benefits. As soon as a project comes outside these tolerance limits, it needs to be escalated. In the workshop you can give a moment's thought together.
"Is the scope of the project clear enough, with all steering committee members and project manager?" Check question "What is the scope?", does it match the contract or mandate.
Another question can be "When does the steering committee meet?".
Agree in your calendar on principal dates and only meet when needed.
And also "How much mandate does the project manager have, what are the tolerance limits in terms of time, money and budget?".
Also make agreements about the report (when does the steering committee want this?).
You can also point out to the steering committee that they are solely responsible for the accuracy of information in the project report. This is not always known by everyone.
Redirecting exceptions must often happen quickly. Does everyone know how to easily reach each other? And especially "how easily can the project executive be reached by the project manager?". Can the project manager call and drop by at all times when needed?

Extra questions may be:
- Which project products/outcomes are being transferred to management (the client)?
- Which products must the client sign off on for approval?
- Who at the client signs for approval?
- What are the acceptance criteria?
- Are there dependencies with other projects?

During the workshop you will not get an answer to every question straight away, you can give these as homework. Of course you record everything in an actions and decisions register. A PMO employee can also facilitate this.

11.2 Template: Workshop intake form

> This form helps the facilitator with preparing for a workshop.
> Write in here a brief description of the workshop (main theme, what are the people invited for?).

Explore – What?	
Reason (causes, context, history)	*What is the reason for the workshop?*
Purpose workshop?	*What needs to be achieved when the workshop has taken place?*
Has this been done before? (experiences)	*A workshop or other interactive meeting?*
Is there sufficient mandate and budget to carry out the outcomes?	*And I mean the workshop outcomes.*

Explore – Who?	
Owner issue (client)	*Who is the client of the workshop?*
What is the interest of the client?	*What does the client of the workshop want to achieve and which other interests play a role?*
Vision client on the workshop as intervention?	*This can also be a feeling or experiences.*
Who are the participants (roles)?	*Make a list of participants, including role description, function and any other useful information.*
Relationship between client & participants?	
Facilitator(s)?	*Who is/are facilitating?*
Others involved?	

Explore – How? (design criteria and global approach)	
Duration workshop	*How much time is needed for the workshop?*
Realistic term	*Time is required to properly prepare and organise a workshop. Is there enough time?*

11.2 Template: Workshop intake form

Explore – How? (design criteria and global approach)	
Location	Sub rooms are needed, tables/chairs setup, catering, projector, other facilities needed?
Is preparation of participants needed?	If so, what homework, how? (reading, training, making,…)

Preparing: roadmap (workshop design)

Time	Duration	Purpose	Method & tips	Who

Preparation checklist
- (Have) Organise(d) facility services like: space, parking, food, drinks.
- Send invitation.
- Send possible homework assignment.
- Design for setup of the workshop space (tables and chairs).
- Organise requirements like: workshop material, documentation, reference work, internet.
- Photo camera (to capture).

Follow-up (after the workshop)	
Who is responsible for the follow-up communication?	Can be the client or manager, however does not need to be.
What will be communicated?	Which information?
How and when will be communicated?	After how many days, in what form (medium)? One or multiple times?
Who will monitor the follow-up of the actions?	
Follow-up meeting yes/no?	If so: when, with whom and where? Will all the participants of the workshop be there, or just a selection? Will the other participants agree when it is a selection?

12. SIZE MATTERS. HOW MANY ARE NEEDED FOR THE PMO?

A project is only as strong as its weakest link.

The basic principle is that a pop-up PMO offers support and process improvements to the project or the programme. It is sometimes about a small-scale construction project, or sometimes about a long-term quality improvement programme. Depending on the complexity and duration of the project, more or less PMO activities will be needed. Is 1 FTE sufficient for this activity to be provided now or is that already too much or not enough? How do you determine the size of a pop-up PMO?

A method for calculating the necessary PMO staffing is to start from the time that is needed for a certain task/function. These tasks can be put in a spreadsheet and an estimation can be made of the required time to:
1. Set up (start-up).
2. Execute a controlled progress.

This can then be translated to the type of PMO employee what is/are required in terms of tasks or specialisation.

Example of fictitious PMO staffing calculation
(can also be used for a permanent PMO)

Task:	#Hours for setting up:	Hours per week controlled progress:
Stakeholder management & communication	80	8
Planning	80	
Resource management	60	8
Benefit management	0	0
Reporting	24	4
Risk management	40	4
Issue management	10	8
Change control	32	4
Finance *(including prognosis)*	80	8
Quality management	50	18
Information and configuration management *(including filing)*	32	24
Transition management (transfer to management organisation)	8	1
Knowledge management	8	1

12. SIZE MATTERS. HOW MANY ARE NEEDED FOR THE PMO?

Task:	#Hours for setting up:	Hours per week controlled progress:
Secretariat *(includes submitting plans and minutes, facilitating training, excludes schedules meeting rooms for project employees)*	5	8
Total number of hours (per week)	509	88
Conclusion	12 weeks (with 1 FTE)	2,2 FTE per week

Variables that affect the amount of PMO hours are:
- How many sub teams or sub projects will the project include (how many (sub) project managers will there be supported, how many sub schedules will be created and maintained)?
- How many parties (both internal and external) are involved?
- Which tasks will the PMO execute (standard, optional, how extensive)?
- How many products will the project deliver?
- How often are status updates and financial reports required?
- How often is it desirable to hold a certain meeting whereby support is required, should minutes be taken?
- How many resources within the project are expected and what are the tasks for this?
- Which tooling is available and what needs to be done manually?

There may be many more questions like these. The point is that the PMO employee has to try and find out what the demands of the environment will be towards the temporary PMO. See also appendix B 'Intake form between project manager and PMO employee'.

With the elaborated overview of time spent, the PMO employee is ready to take on the next meeting with the project manager. He will have to give approval for the number of hours required to set up the temporary PMO within the agreed timeframe and to agree on the number of FTEs in terms of utilisation for the controlled progress. Of course this also depends on the available budget and the contractual agreements. It is therefore of importance to involve the PMO in an early stage to include this role in the budget calculation.

With a shortage of budget, it can for instance be decided to take twice as long on setting up the temporary PMO (consequently, for example, status reports will be available later) or it can be decided to perform tasks less intensively (for example a less strict quality control). Or return tasks to the project manager, who then has to execute these himself.

After final agreement on the task package, the PMO employee can define actions to recruit the right people and to start constructing the pop-up PMO.

12. SIZE MATTERS. HOW MANY ARE NEEDED FOR THE PMO?

An option to consider is to, for the setup of the temporary PMO, also deploy senior (mostly more expensive) PMO employees who, once the services and processes are established, hand this over to more junior employees. By means of (part time) coaching of the junior employees and regular meetings with the project manager, a grip can be kept on the quality and continuity of the PMO activities.

If the organisation is at a Maturity level 2 or 3 (of the P3M3® model), all functions can be executed in accordance with the following PMO size overview:

Number of Programme / Project employees	30	60	120	200	300	500	1000
Number of PMO employees	3	4	7	9	12	17	25
% PMO employees	10	7	6	5	4	3	3

Source: P3O

N.B. this model is based on:
- All programmes, projects and meetings in one location.
- Few third parties.
- A simple financial model and report.
- Clear number of stakeholders and types and means of communication.
- Stable programme and support situation (at the start-up more support is required, at the end of the programme possibly less).

13. PMO EMPLOYEE COMPETENCES & PERSONAL GOALS

People with goals succeed because they know where they are going...
It's as simple as that.
Earl Nightingale

PMO is a profession that is developing rapidly. In the Netherlands not long ago it was merely seen as a step up to project manager. In countries like America, Australia and England the PMO profession is more developed. There the project managers are a part of a central permanent PMO and as a project manager you can grow on to management positions in the PMO.

In the Netherlands and England several companies and organisations have developed career and function models for PMO. Useful models are:
1. IPMA NCB
2. APMG P3O
3. Ordina
4. KPN Consulting

Please contact me if you know more models.

1. IPMA NCB

The IPMA book "Competence profiles, Certification levels and Functions in the Project Management and Project Support Field" written by Jan Willem Donselaar, Bert Hedeman and Henny Portman appeared in December 2011. In this book a lot of attention is given to various PMO functions.

		Project				Portfolio		Programme		
		Simple	Average	Complex	Extreme			Complex	Average	Simple
A					Project Director	Portfolio director		Senior programme manager		
B			Senior project manager	Head project office	PM consultant	Head of PMO	Head programme office	programme manager		
C		Project manager	Head project office	Senior PMO officer	PM specialist	Senior PMO officer	Senior PMO officer	Head programme office	Process manager	
D		Team manager	PMO officer	PMO officer	PMO officer	PMO officer	PMO officer	PMO officer	PMO officer	PMO officer
E		PMO assistant	PMO assistant	PMO assistant	PMO assistant	PMO assistant	PMO assistant	PMO assistant	PMO assistant	PMO assistant

This book contributes enormously in getting the PMO field of expertise to become insightful and mature. Project manager and PMO employee are equal positions. Below a brief description of the various PMO functions.

Level E
- PMO assistant: is capable to support the project, programme or portfolio management team for a limited number of PMO services under supervision.

Level D
- PMO employee: is capable to support the project, programme or portfolio management team for all PMO services.

Level C
- PMO specialist: is capable to independently support the project, programme or portfolio management team in a limited number of services and to contribute to further developing the project, programme and portfolio management field of expertise. Develops "best practices".
- Senior PMO employee: is capable to independently support the project, programme and portfolio management team in all PMO services and can function in extreme projects and programmes.
- Head project or programme office (PMO manager): is capable to set up and manage the PMO and can function as head project or programme office for complex projects and average complex programmes.

Level B
- PM consultant: is capable to independently support the project, programme and portfolio management team for all PMO services within the entire field of expertise of project management and to lead the development of the field of expertise (PMO expert).
- Head project or programme office, Head PMO (PMO manager): is capable to set up and manage the PMO and can function as a portfolio manager, head of a project office for very complex projects or head of a programme office for a complex programme.

Level A
- Project or portfolio director: experienced manager who can lead in complex organisations and can manage on behalf of management a very complex project or the project portfolio.

Next figure is an interpretation of possible career paths with a reference to the IPMA certification levels.

13. PMO EMPLOYEE COMPETENCES & PERSONAL GOALS

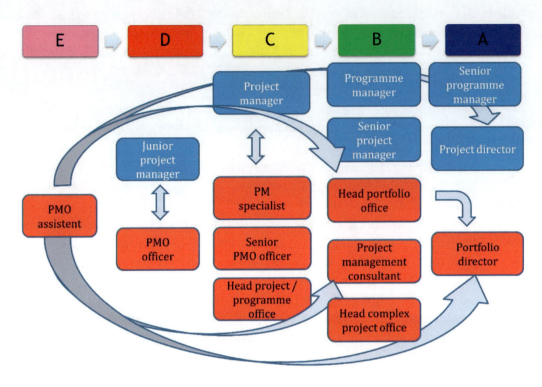

Figure 13.1 Possible career paths in the project management field of expertise

> The following functions are possible in a pop-up PMO:
> - PMO assistant. Provides a limited number of services in a project or programme under direct supervision.
> - (Senior) PMO employee. Provides all required supporting services in a project or programme. Independently, if senior.
> - Project management (PM) specialist. Is fully specialised in certain PMO services and develops best practices for this. For example a project controller, risk manager or planner. See for more examples the overview of the P3O specialist roles in the next paragraph.
> - Head of a (complex) project or programme office. Can set this up and manage.
> - Project management (PM) consultant. Can independently support and manage developments of best practices.

PMO employees, project management specialists and project and programme managers can, if necessary, be deployed from a permanent PMO within an organisation (a sort of internal rental to projects).

13. PMO EMPLOYEE COMPETENCES & PERSONAL GOALS

There are also functions within permanent PMOs like head project or programme office or portfolio office and portfolio director.

2. APMG P3O

In appendix A of the P3O, 21 roles are being discussed that exercise (part of) a PMO. These are divided into 2 types of areas: 1. Management and generic roles, 2. Functional or specialist roles. P3O is based on a "pick and mix" principle and purposely calls it roles instead of functions. This allows for a profile to be made to fit, depending on the required demand.

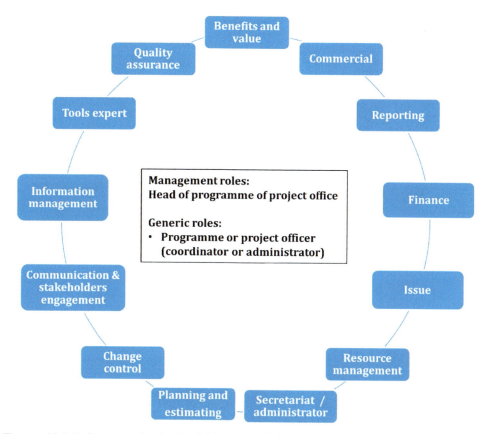

Figure 13.2 Relevant roles in the P3O methodology

1. **Management and generic functions**
   These are functions or roles like:
   - Head of a project or programme office (pop-up PMO).
   - Project or programme officer.

   The P3O/PMO sponsor is also mentioned, this is a precondition for the setup of the entire P3O model including permanent and pop-up PMOs.

13. PMO EMPLOYEE COMPETENCES & PERSONAL GOALS

2. Functional or specialist roles

A senior PMO employee can specialise in a specific project management field of expertise or in multiple fields. Such a specialisation is similar to the IPMA function of project management specialist (level C). For example, think of the following possibilities:

- Project coordinator or planner.
- Information and configuration manager.
- Change management coordinator.
- Financial controller.
- Communication manager.
- Project management consultant.
- Benefit manager.
- Issue manager.
- Quality manager or Quality Assurance officer.
- Resource manager.
- Risk manager.
- Report employee (reporting).
- Tooling expert (training in and support of project management related software tools).

A specialist is an expert in the concerning role, is proactive in that field and promotes methods, standards and best practices for this. The specialist keeps informed through events, books, forums, publishes himself and possibly provides training in this field. Specialists can also monitor processes in projects and programmes and offer consultancy services. Consultancy can include advice, coaching, reviews, the facilitating of workshops and the guiding of project and programme managers in setting up the processes.

3. Ordina model:

For the role of PMO employee Ordina uses a growth model, build up from three levels of generic PMO roles and growth to three specialist roles. Besides a division of tasks based on the PMO services (the services that PMO provides), the knowledge and function level of the employees are being considered.

13. PMO EMPLOYEE COMPETENCES & PERSONAL GOALS

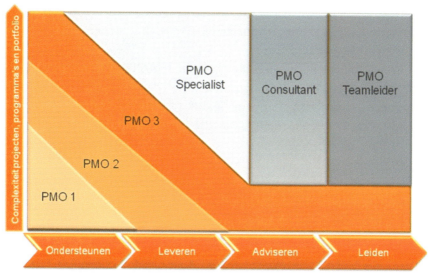

Figure 13.3 PMO roles (Ordina, unit PMO)

One can evolve from an executing PMO role (support and deliver) to a specialisation in a particular service, towards consultancy regarding the applicability of services or towards a managing role.

4. **KPN Consulting model:**

A distinction is made in 5 types of PMO employees, where the functions are compared to the IPMA competence model.

Project PA	Junior PMO employee	Med PMO employee	Senior PMO officer Head of PMO	Head PMO PM(O) consultant
Calendars Minutes Various other tasks	Look after the shop of a running temporary or fixed PMO	Proactively determines the projects governance and aligns this with the organization	Comes with proposals of how to improve the project(s) governance within projects & organisations. Or specialist in particular PMO function.	Manages multiple PMO employees within project, programme or organisation. Or portfolio manager. Or consultant project management.
	The project manager asks, the PMO employee does	Sparring partner of project managers	Sparring partner of directors, controllers, project managers	Sparring partner of directors, controllers, project managers
Secretarial training	IPMA E/D	IPMA D IPMA B (with complex projects and programmes)	IPMA D/C/B	IPMA C/B

PMO career options →

Figure 13.4 PMO roles (KPN Consulting)

13. PMO EMPLOYEE COMPETENCES & PERSONAL GOALS

Market perspective:
Own research has shown that there are, per market area, major differences visible in the level of maturity of the PMO.
In some market areas, such as industry (amongst which building companies) and banking in the financial sector, the PMO work has long been recognised (sometimes under different names), these areas know permanent PMOs that deliver services to projects. In other market areas, especially in health care and education, PMO is still very premature or absent.

There where PMO exists already for some time, people seem to focus per market on a few processes and functions of the PMO, both in temporary and permanent PMOs. In the health care and educational sectors, PMO is still in its infancy.

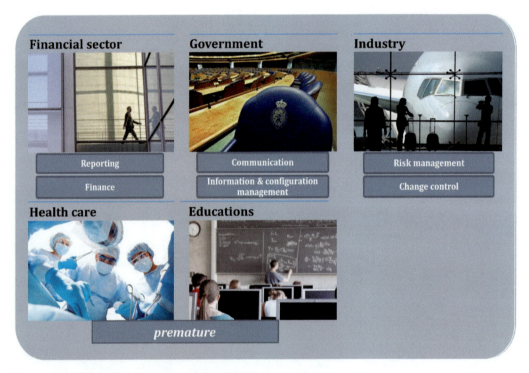

Figure 13.5 Main focus areas per market

13. PMO EMPLOYEE COMPETENCES & PERSONAL GOALS

Which competences and experience does a (senior) PMO employee need?

As a PMO employee it is useful when you have the following experience:
- A financial background.
- Experience in planning (and planning tools).
- Recruitment experience (be able to make a pre selection of new project employees).
- Service management (you recognise project management processes quicker).
- In the project management field of expertise (PMO employee is not a step up to project management, it is a separate discipline).

And, according to the IPMA book "Competence profiles, Certification levels and Functions in the Project Management and Project Support Field", the following qualities at level D and C for a (senior) PMO employee:
- Take initiative.
- Be able to persuade and deal with doubt.
- Communicative skills (listening, concluding, writing).
- Manage individual employees and distributed processes.
- Sense of responsibility.
- Quality focused.
- Focused on detail.
- Be able to collaborate in heterogeneous teams and wider work relations.
- Likes researching (learning orientation and being able to analyse problems).
- Be able to form a judgement.
- Be stress resistant.
- Have environmental awareness (have knowledge of organisation and organisation sensitivity).

It is moreover of importance to have experience with project management.

13.1 Personal learning goals

You are solely responsible for the success of your career. In order to develop yourself you will need to push boundaries and have or get an idea of your future. And both are not always as easy. What do you want in terms of career? Do you want to continue with what you do now? Do you want to specialise yourself? Do you want to go towards a management role? Or do want to advise? Anything is possible. When you do not know your career goal, it may help to find out what drives you. What gives you energy?

The pyramid of McLelland establishes a relationship between the visible qualities of employees, the knowledge and skills, and the self-image, hidden below the surface, motives, characteristics and norms and values. The model lets you think about what your strong points are, what you really want and how you can achieve this.

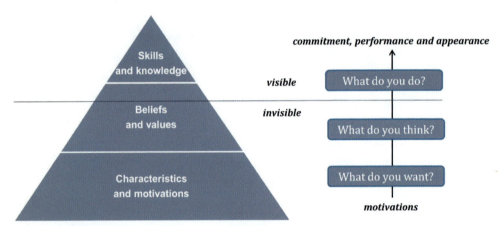

Figure 13.6 The Pyramid (or iceberg model) of McLelland

What do you want?
To get this clear, you can ask yourself questions like:
- What do I enjoy?
- What gives me pleasure and satisfaction in my work and life?
- What do I want to do the most? What motivates me?
- What drives me?
- What do I find important in my work and life?
- Where do I see myself in ten years?
- What do I want to achieve in life?

13.1 Personal learning goals

Ask yourself a why question seven times.
Start with "why would I want to be a PMO employee (or project manager)?" Look at your answer and ask yourself the question again, why did you give that answer, why is that important? Do this seven times. It is likely that after the last question you have found your inner motivation. By repeatedly asking "Why?", you get a deeper insight in the underlying motivations. If you do not ask the why often enough, you will only find an explanation and not the main reason.

What do you think?
To gain insight into your current motivation, you can ask yourself the following questions:
- What am I good at?
- What do people appreciate in me?
- Which tasks would I like to have in a function and which function would fit that?
- What do I find important in a function?
- When am I disappointed?
- What do I find important in working with a project manager and team?
- How would I want to be treated?
- What can make me angry?
- What blocks me (do I have inner obstacles or believes)?

Having arrived at this point, it should immediately be clear to you how you look at what you are doing now. Are you a PMO employee and do you want to further develop yourself in this? If so, which direction? Towards PMO management or a specialisation? Are you project manager and do you want to manage more complex projects or programmes or do you want to continue growing towards a head PMO function?

What do you do? What are you going to do?
At the questions above, the main objective was to get insight into your knowledge, skills, inner motivations, motives, norms, values and beliefs. Now you can draw yourself a sort of personal plan of action. Here you can define actions for yourself on the basis of 3 types of questions:
1. Do I have sufficient knowledge?
2. Do I have sufficient skills?
3. Does my attitude require any adjustment?

1. Knowledge:
- Do I know enough to get started?
- Do I know what I should do?
- Do I have enough information?
- Where can I find more information?

13.1 Personal learning goals

- What kind of training could I do?
- Which books, blogs or sites could I read?

2. Skills:
- Can I do it?
- What will I do?
- Do my actions have any effect?
- Do I have the abilities to carry it out?
- How will I further develop my required skills?

3. Attitude:
- How do I think I come across to others?
- Dare I?
- Do I want to?
- What is keeping me?

By now you should have gained some more insight into yourself. A good coach can help you with this. The next step is to determine what you need in order to further develop yourself.

1. Which training, courses, workshops, seminars and so forth will help you?
2. Which networks, clubs, organisations will you visits?
3. Which books and blogs will you read?
4. Which type of projects would you like?
5. Which type of project managers and or PMO employees would you like to work with?
6. How will you express what you want?

13.2 Profiling helps you achieve your goals

To achieve your goals you will have to give a moment's thought to how you will profile yourself. "Beat your own drum" as the Americans say. Which means so much as; make sure you show yourself. Become aware of your talents and ensure that others see them too. In countries like the Netherlands, the culture there is that people are inclined to see this as 'bragging'. However, profiling yourself has nothing to do with bragging!
Profiling means to characterise yourself and to show your distinctiveness. People who are good at profiling themselves, pull success towards them. Just delivering quality is not enough! You should especially teach yourself to 'sell'.

See yourself as a product that needs to be sold and reflect on the following aspects:
1. Visual (package)
2. Content
3. Marketing

1. Visual (package):
A famous study by Albert Mehrabian shows the effect of verbal and non-verbal communication on how someone judges you. In his experiments he discovered that someone's opinion about the other was determined for 55% by how someone looked and behaved (visual and non-verbal behaviour), for 38% by how someone said something (vocal, the voice, tone and thus auditory behaviour) and for only 7% by what someone said (verbal, content and words).

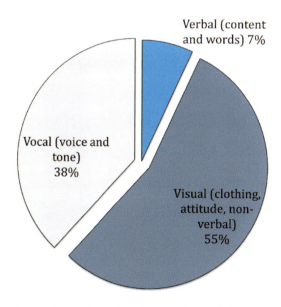

Figure 13.7 Three V rule by Albert Mehrabian

13.2 Profiling helps you achieve your goals

Especially with a first contact (where you make a first impression) it is useful to reflect on this. Also when you go and introduce yourself to the project team or when you are facing a group. Think carefully about how you want to come across and adapt yourself accordingly. Attitude (how do you sit or stand), clothing (yes or no jacket) and facial expression (smile or no smile).

2. Content:
Despite the 'three V rule' of Albert Mehrabian, it is important to make clear what your expertise is. With which issues and problems can you help? What can people call or e-mail you for?

3. Marketing yourself:
Whether or not you are employed totally does not matter when it comes to the importance of selling yourself. And with selling I mean ensuring that people see you and recognise you for your ability and knowledge. Make yourself visible.

Personal branding is a tool for this. This is presenting yourself to others as a brand, whereby you evoke positive images and associations. You use your personality, knowledge and experience to make you stand out. You show your employer and clients who you are and what you stand for.

People do business with people. When you are looking for a new job, client or project, it is good to profile yourself. That a CV should be up to date speaks for itself. More important is to adapt your CV with every potential assignment to the need. Emphasise what is needed and write your motivation so that it fits the company or project in question.

Nowadays a lot of information is being found online. Online visibility and profiling is becoming more and more important.

Google and social media platforms largely determine your (online) reputation. When someone wants to know who you are, they will google you or look for you on business media platforms.
The results Google shows can make or break your reputation. Know what can be found and read about you online!

13.3 Seven tips for personal profiling

1. Which strengths, talents, skills, passions and values do you have? List them for yourself. Which make you unique and distinctive?

2. Consider how you want others to see you. How do you want to come across? Do you want to be remembered as the good quality controller, a good organiser, the planner who also has an understanding of risk management or would you rather be seen as an expert in the field of project governance? When you know how you want to be seen, you can work on that and make sure that people are actually going to see you that way! Also think about a specialty: with what subject do you want people to immediately think of you? What is your specialty, or what specialty do you want to further develop, so that, in future, people think of you when they need somebody in that field of expertise? To determine a specialty may perhaps seem restrictive, however, it does give you a much better focus. This will pay more in the long run.

3. Show yourself. For example, blog about yourself or about your field of expertise, and show who you are and what you stand for. Twitter and LinkedIn are also possible means where you can profile yourself. Be relevant and ensure that your skills and knowledge area(s) correspond to current matters in project country and keep your knowledge and information updated. Collect and take part in information sources that are of relevance to you and accordingly also share that knowledge with the people you meet through your blog, meetings or other media.

4. Make sure that your profiles have been updated on various sites and social media platforms. Have you got a photo of yourself everywhere? An automatic signature can also tell a lot. Even a missing photo and profile says something.

5. Create your own elevator pitch. At a meeting someone asks you what you do. What will you reply? A good elevator pitch is made up of the following schedule:

13.3 Seven tips for personal profiling

Key message (1 sentence):	"I ...." <what do you do / look for / want>
Explanation/ justification:	"By that I mean ..." <Further explanation of what you want, are looking for, how you intend to achieve that>
Example:	"Remember ... It is just like ..." <Mention qualities that you have successfully used in the past>
Key message:	"In short ..." "So, if you are looking for someone who ..... I will be at your service"

Speaking for 1 minute is approximately 150 words.

6. Do not go and wait to show what you stand for. Seize opportunities, call on your own opportunities in life that reflect what you stand for, publish about your field of expertise and your unique perspective on it. Share your vision with people you get to talk to, listen carefully and try to think of how you, from your personal brand, can help this person in the best possible way.

7. Give and you shall receive. Some people struggle with the idea of giving "free" knowledge away. You can always give away knowledge, help somebody with your knowledge or clarify a situation with the help of your talents. This way you build up your personal brand in a natural way, without having to wait for an assignment to prove yourself. Of course, you do not have to be a free service provider; keep a good balance. To give something of yourself is commercially very healthy, however, giving yourself away is not.

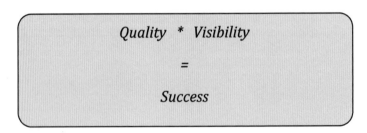

*Quality * Visibility*

=

Success

14. PROJECT MANAGER AND PMO EMPLOYEE; THE GOLDEN DUO

Management is doing things right; leadership is doing the right things.
(Peter F. Drucker)

With a pop-up PMO, the collaboration between a project manager and PMO employee is challenging and exciting. As the relationship needs to be build up and become clear in a very short time. The better the relationship, the better the project control and thus also likely the project outcome.

You could also compare this collaboration with a restaurant.
In a restaurant you have a good chef and a host, working effectively together in order to achieve a Michelin star. Both are in the same field of expertise, however, have different competences. Both need to have confidence in each other and have the courage to let go of matters.

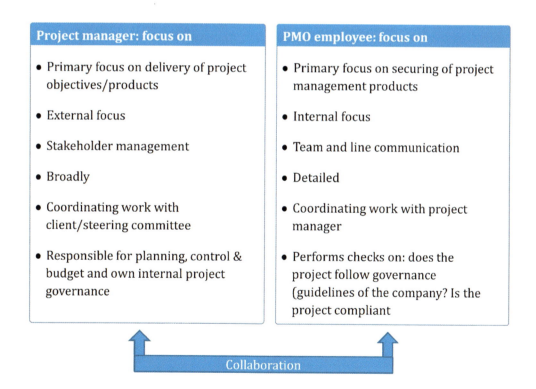

Figure 14.1 Focus area differences between project manager and PMO employee

14. PROJECT MANAGER AND PMO EMPLOYEE; THE GOLDEN DUO

In general you can identify a number of levels in which for each level a task package is being handed over to the PMO employee.

Level	Project manager	Pop-up PMO
0	Does everything himself.	There is no supporter.
1	Outsource administrative work.	PA (Personal Assistant).
2	Outsource some tasks. Keeps full control. Needs to manage the temporary PMO team himself.	Junior. Takes on some tasks at the request of project manager.
3	Can let go of a lot of work. A lot is being taken out of hands, without having to ask for it.	Mid. Proactively takes on a lot of tasks from the project manager.
4	Gets advice on project governance. The temporary PMO team is being set up for him/her.	Senior. Helps setting up the project governance and processes. With a pop-up PMO of multiple people, setting these up (who does what, when).
5	Level 4 + outsourcing management and monitoring of team.	Coach or consultant. Full sparring partner of the project manager.

With the aforementioned list, a qualifying statement is made about the task package of a pop-up PMO. This PMO can consist of one or more people. A PMO employee of level 1 requires less expertise than a PMO employee of level 2 and for level 2 in turn less than a PMO employee of level 3 etc.

The setting up of a pop-up PMO once is not sufficient. Depending on the (increasing or decreasing) task package during the project, will again and again have to be considered to what extent the available expertise is in line with the modified task package.

14.1 Captainitis

What if a PMO employee detects something, however is afraid to say it to the project manager? Unthinkable? In practice, I find that this happens a lot. Not only in projects, also in aviation it can happen that a co-pilot does not intervene when the captain is likely to take a wrong-headed decision.

March 27, 1977 fog was emerging at the airport of Tenerife (Canary Islands).
A KLM-Boeing 747 taxis to the runway. A Pan Am-Boeing has to take off after KLM and is on his way to a turning point via the runway. The KLM pilots are in a hurry, because with delay their maximum allowed number of hours will likely be exceeded. The control tower gives permission for the flight, however not yet for starting. The density of the fog increases and approaches the start limit. The KLM co-pilot begins repeating the flight permission, whilst he is still busy with that, captain Jacob Veldhuyzen van Zanten announces "We are going…". He disengages the brakes and hits the accelerator. The KLM co-pilot hurriedly finishes his repeat text for permission and says: "and we are now at take-off". This is an unusual order and the control tower confirms with: "OK, standby for take-off". But because at the same time the Pan-Am reports to the control tower that they are still on the runway, KLM only hears a whistle instead of the message from the control tower. They do not hear the "OK, standby for take-off". 5 seconds later the control tower asks the Pan-Am whether they have left the runway.
The KLM flight engineer hears this and asks the captain "He has left right, that Pan-Am?" Of course, says the captain, whilst already at full speed.
The answer of Pan-Am to the control tower "No, we are still on the runway" could not be given anymore. At that moment the ascending KLM aeroplane crashes into the Pan-Am plane.

Why did the co-pilot not intervene (he was right in his mind)? There were 3 moments when he could have.
1. When the captain said: "We are going", whilst he was still checking the permission for the flight.
2. When the captain disengaged the brakes and hit the accelerator before "clearance" was given.
3. When he heard the KLM engineer asking whether Pan-Am had actually left the runway.

14.1 Captainitis

At the accident in Tenerife, the "not acting" of the co-pilot had fatal consequences.

This phenomenon is in aviation called "Captainitis[19] [20]". Captainitis implies that one should not doubt somebody because of his authority.

The same phenomenon you see regularly in the relationship between a project manager and a PMO employee.

Tips for the project manager: Do not be afraid to once in a while be open to your PMO employee. Occasionally ask for reflection and say afterwards "thank you". Do not enter into a discussion, you may only continue asking. It will help you in achieving your project outcomes.

Also dare to delegate.
- You do not have to be a perfectionist, not everyone can be good at everything, that is impossible.
- When you think you can do better yourself, set yourself up as teacher/coach, give the other person time to learn. Provide support where needed. What is better than a successful student who tells you in subsequent years that he owes a lot to you.
- You will not be less important when you hand over tasks, rather the other way round.
- Giving up the idea that you have to be an expert in everything, requires confidence in yourself and your PMO employee.

Tips for the PMO employee: Listen to that little voice inside you more often. Dare to speak your doubts about something to the project managers. Tell your message in the I-form (avoid offensive words like "you").

---

[19] Pacelle van Goethem, IJsverkopen aan eskimo's (de psychologie van overtuigen) ("Selling ice cream to the Eskimos" Only available in Dutch)
[20] Shari Frisinger "Captainitis" on youtube

14.2　The fear to delegate

When you ask a project manager why he does certain tasks himself and not delegates them to you, you expect a variety of answers.
Robert Nelson's book "Empowering Employees Through Delegation" gives a top 10 of excuses for not having to delegate:

10. I love to be busy and like to take my own decisions.
9. I am worried about the lack of control over the performances of my employee when I delegate.
8. My employee is not yet experienced enough to take on more responsibilities.
7. My employee is busy enough already.
6. My employee is a specialist and lacks the overall knowledge to take certain decisions.
5. There are tasks that I just do not delegate.
4. My position as project manager enables me to get things done quicker.
3. I cannot afford a mistake of an employee. This would cost me too much.
2. It costs me more time to explain it than to do it quickly myself.
1. My employee has not enough experience yet.

What a surprise: of course the employee has little experience when the project manager does not give him the opportunity to spread his wings!

Delegating is difficult, because it means that you give up a little bit of control. You can give your project manager a number of hints in the form of:
- If you as project manager think that you are the only one capable to execute certain tasks, you will always remain stuck in your current level of work.
- A person who is not replaceable, can therefore also not be promoted.
- The most valuable managers (for an organisation) are those who train and coach others.
- Dare to delegate is an essential leadership quality.
- The project manager can focus on the tasks that are really important for him as manager.
- And see further in chapter 5.1 (added value of a PMO employee within a project).

Pitfalls for project managers when delegating:
Delegating calls for an investment of the project manager as executive. Often it will, in the short term, be more attractive for him or her to do it themselves. It will be done quicker then and he/she knows for certain that it meets its own requirements. On the other hand: if the project manager never hands over a task, he will always have to execute this task himself.

14.2 The fear to delegate

Delegating costs time, however in that time you train an employee to become a good and valuable PMO employee.

Managers are often perfectionists and have therefore difficulty letting go, especially when they are too involved in the content of the project: with the risk of constantly watching someone closely or interfering with how something is being executed outside the agreed moments. The result is that the other loses his self-confidence and motivation.

If the project manager judges too much from his own (high) standards when discussing the results, he/she deprives the other of the enjoyment in his/her work. The project manager has to give space and accept small mistakes. In other words: give the other the chance to learn.

15. FOUR TIMES PASSION FOR PMO

Above all, be true to yourself, and if you cannot put your heart in it, take yourself out of it.
Hardy D. Jackson

What is it with PMO employees? The people who consciously choose for this relatively new profession characterise themselves as people with a certain passion. An enthusiasm that shows itself in being helpful, well-informed, like to solve organisational problems, want to create transparency and have an eye for the stakeholders around a project. The real project manager can also be recognised by his or her passion for that profession.

Suppose you still doubt whether the PMO profession is it for you, you can then have a look at the following four critical aspects of passion[21]:
1. Purpose
2. Pleasure
3. Problems
4. Personal

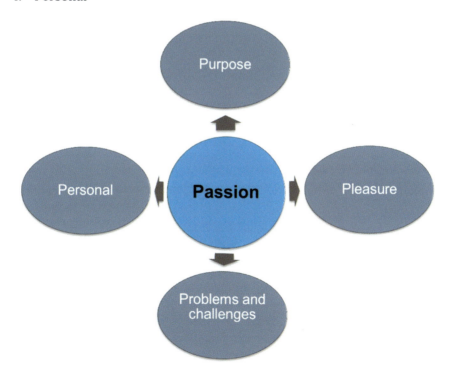

---

[21] Business driven PMO setup (Mark Price Perry)

15. FOUR TIMES PASSION FOR PMO

Almost everyone has a certain passion for a hobby or sport. How about the work that you do or want to do?

1. Purpose:
People are driven by nature because of a purpose or plan. Unlike other organisational functions like sales people who are driven by rewards and performance, PMO employees are often driven by something within. PMO employees usually work in the background, many activities and results often remain unnoticed. Without an inner sense of a plan or purpose there cannot be passion.
Which purpose do you pursue in your work?

2. Pleasure:
Passion and pleasure are closely related. It is very important to enjoy a passion. That does not mean that the goal of a passion is having pleasure, it does mean that there is an opportunity to make it pleasurable.
What makes you happy in your work?

3. Problems:
It is not enough to have a purpose and pleasure in what you do. There is more needed to keep a passion. The solving of a problem or the conquering of an obstacle is also a part of passion. When you feel passionate about something, you want to become better at it, you want to take on challenges and be challenged. The satisfaction you feel after overcoming something difficult is also a part of your passion.
Which challenge do you want to take on in your next project? Or what would you like to improve in your organisation?

4. Personal:
Passion is something very personal and acknowledges and reminds you of who you are. People with passion for their work know who they are and to what they contribute. There is a certain pride in what you do.
Which aspect of your work and how you contribute to this, are you proud of?

> Passion is the fuel for success. Passion gives motivation, energy and strength. And takes you faster to your goal. Without passion there is little happening which is really significant.

15. FOUR TIMES PASSION FOR PMO

General characteristics of passion are:
- You would also do the work for less or no reward or salary.
- You are looking for opportunities to do more than just what is being asked. You want to continuously improve yourself and become better in your profession.
- You feel a better person if your work has been received satisfactorily.
- You do not take time into account and it does not matter that you spend more time than is agreed.
- You receive your salary for who you are and not on the basis of the position you occupy.

Signals that indicate a lack of passion are:
- You do your work just for the money.
- You are especially focused on your reputation.
- To finish the job is the most important, not the process there or how well you achieve this result.
- You look for ways to finish your tasks as quickly as possible, so that you can soon do something else again.
- You are too busy running around and do not take time for yourself, both psychologically and mentally.

Keep your passion alive:
All over the world the PMO profession is booming and the first successes are emerging. More and more PMO related literature is being published and the number of companies offering PMO services is increasing.
Not everyone sees this yet and debate will often occur.
The trick is to not let your emotions be sucked towards those of difficult people and people who do not want to understand it. Shrug your shoulders, keep smiling and hold on to your longer term goals and plan.
Do your work passionately and carry it out.

> *"Great artists aren't great because of their technique;*
>
> *they are great because of their passion."*

15. FOUR TIMES PASSION FOR PMO

OVERVIEW TEMPLATES AND CHECKLISTS

Checklists:
- Intake form between project manager and PMO employee (Appendix B) — 186
- PMO closure checklist (Appendix E) — 202
- PMO setup checklist (Appendix D) — 197
- Review tips — 111

Templates:
- Decision register — 141
- Change register — 101
- Issue register — 95
- Quality register — 115
- Lessons learned register — 135
- Onboarding project employees example — 69
- Pop-up PMO objectives and agreements (Appendix C) — 196
- Resources hire register — 70
- Risk register — 88
- Stakeholder matrix — 54
- Workshop intake form — 151

APPENDIX A: GLOSSARY

Accountable	Responsible. The one who has final responsibility, authority and gives approval to the result. If it comes down to it, he/she needs to be able to make the final judgement, have veto power. There is just one person Accountable.
Audit	Inspection of a (process) organisation (part). A project audit gives the project sponsor, client, project manager and project team an interim overview of what has gone well and what needs to be improved in order for the project to be successfully completed.
Balanced Scorecard	The Balanced Scorecard (BSC) is a model with which the performances of an organisation, a team etc. can be assessed in a balanced way. Measurement is central.
Benefit	Measurable improvement resulting from a project or programme outcome and perceived as an advantage by one or more stakeholders.
Best practice	A technique, work method, process or activity which has proven itself as being effective. The theory is that with the right work method, a project can be executed with fewer problems, fewer unforeseen complications and better outcomes. For organisations it is important to know the "best practice" within their industry and to benchmark their own work method with it. A project that has been successful in a certain way, serves as "best practice" for new projects.
Budget	An authorised amount or combination of amounts for achieving a result.
Business as Usual (BAU)	The usual execution of the activities within an organisation.
Business case	The business justification of the investment decision.
Centre of Excellence (COE) - Knowledge center	A corporate coordinating function for portfolios, programmes and projects providing standards, consistency of methods and processes, knowledge management, assurance and training.
Change	A change of a formally defined status. Mostly of scope, time, quality or money.

Appendix A: Glossary

Compliance	Term which indicates that a person or organisation is operating in compliance with the applicable laws and regulations and in accordance with all agreements internally and externally made by an organisation. It is about meeting standards or to comply with them.
Exception	Situation in which it is expected that the tolerance levels agreed between project manager and steering committee or client, will be exceeded.
Focal point	The person or organisation responsible for the coordination of the activities and tasks between different groups of employees.
Governance (corporate)	Within business administration the term is being used to denote how an organisation should be conducted well, efficiently and responsibly, as well as the accountability of the policy pursued towards stakeholders amongst which the owners (shareholders), employees, customers and the society as a whole. Project governance includes the structures, roles and responsibilities to be able to make decisions in a project. See also chapter 4 "Focus on project objective, governance and result gives project success".
Impact (of risk)	The result of a particular threat or opportunity actually occurring, or the expectation of such a result.
Issue	A relevant event that has happened, was not planned and requires action. It can be any concern, query, request for change, suggestion or off-specification raised during a project.
Iteration	Repetition. Iterative developing is the breaking up of the project into small chunks. With an iterative approach, you go step by step and use your progressing insights in a next phase.
Key Deliverable	Essential, (yet) to deliver product.
Key Performance Indicator (KPI)	Variable to analyse performance of organisations or parts of it.

Appendix A: Glossary

Kick-off	Meeting at the start of the project or a phase within the project to promote effective and efficient execution of the project or phase. Should both lead to common understanding, as to motivation for the assignment. The rules of the game will also be made clear (how do we treat each other, etc.).
Knowledge management	It is an approach that puts the role of knowledge at the centre in the organisation, and has set itself the goal of managing and supporting knowledge work in order to fully utilise the added value of knowledge. Knowledge management has as basis that knowledge and knowledge work can be identified and mapped, that procedures can be developed for generating, managing and applying knowledge, and that knowledge can be recorded in information systems.
Lessons Learned	These are collected and aim to encourage action, so that the positive lessons learned of a project are anchored in the working method of the organisation and the organisation is able to avoid the negative lessons learned at future projects.
Log	Data collection managed by the project manager that does not require agreement by the steering committee regarding format and composition.
Milestone	A significant event in the project that marks the progress of the project. For example the completion of key work packages, products or a particular phase.
Performance monitoring	Identifying what has so far been achieved in comparison to the money spent.
Portfolio	A series of projects and/or programmes that deliver one or more strategic objectives and possibly use the same people and means.
Product backlog	A list of all features, functions, technology, improvements and bug fixes that together describe the changes that will be made to the product in future releases. The items on the product backlog are often displayed as user stories.
Product Breakdown Structure (PBS)	A hierarchy of all the products to be produced during a project.

Appendix A: Glossary

Product description	A description of a product's purpose, composition, derivation and quality criteria. It is produced at planning time, as soon as possible after the need for the product is identified.
Programme	A set of related projects and activities in a temporary organisation in order to deliver predefined objectives that are of strategic importance.
Project Initiation Documentation (PID)	A set of documents that brings together all relevant information necessary to start the project on a sound basis and that is being used to inform all involved in the project.
Quality Assurance (QA)	All planned and systematic activities, implemented within the framework of the quality system and, where needed, to sufficiently demonstrate that the quality standards will be met.
Release	The set of products in a handover. The contents of a release are managed, tested and implemented as a single entity.
Reporting	To deliver an oral or written report.
Request For Change (RFC)	A change of a formally defined status. It is a type of issue.
Requirement	Need or expectation that has been prescribed expressly, apparently or binding.
Resources	Required people and means. All persons, tools, materials and supplies required for providing a particular performance.
Reviewer	A person or group independent of the producer who assesses whether a product meets its requirements as defined in its product description.
Risk	An uncertain event or circumstance which, in future, can occur and the possible negative consequences this has for the project.
Risk appetite	The unique attitude of an organisation towards taking risks that determines which amount of risk it considers as acceptable.
Roadmap	Plan that merges short and long term objectives into specific (technological) solutions with the aim to help achieve those objectives.
Scope	The total of the products to be delivered, the services and to be executed activities.

Appendix A: Glossary

Senior Responsible Owner (SRO)	Person responsible for ensuring that a project or programme meets the objectives and delivers the projected benefits. The SRO should be recognised as the owner throughout the organisation and also have clear authority.
Senior User	The project board/steering committee role responsible for ensuring that the user needs are specified correctly and that the solution meets those needs. Representative of the end user(s).
Stakeholder	Any individual, group or organisation that can influence, be influenced by, or perceives itself to be influenced by an initiative (programme, project, activity or risk).
Team	A (small) number of people (group) that work closely together to achieve a common goal.
Tracking tool	A tool that helps to keep a record of additions and changes.
Transition	The physical transfer of the project result to the client.
Work Breakdown Structure (WBS)	An hierarchic structure in which concrete partial results/products of a project are included. Specific to the WBS is that is indicated who is responsible for what.

APPENDIX B: INTAKE FORM BETWEEN PROJECT MANAGER & PMO EMPLOYEE

1. Inventarisation project & environment

Project or programme	What is the project objective?	*In three sentences.*
	Has the project got a name yet?	*Which?*
	Is it about a project (single business case) or a programme (multiple vision statement)?	
	Which results does the client expect to achieve after execution of the assignment?	*This is the most important benefit, which is sometimes being forgotten in the project/IT news of the day.*
	Is the project/programme cut into logical pieces (in terms of organisation, sub project objectives, locations, plots etc.)?	*Is there an organisation chart yet? Request or else create one as soon as possible.*
Contract	What are the contractual arrangements like? (agreements, money aspects, who does what, time, quality)	*Request and read contract.*
Assignment description	Is there a project mandate or assignment?	*Request and read assignment.*
	Has the assignment been accepted by every stakeholder?	*See also organisation (who are the stakeholders).*
	What is the minimum of products to be delivered?	*Or the product to be delivered.*
	What are the most important milestones?	*Are they already known?*
Time	Planned project duration.	*When does it need to be finished, milestones defined?*
Complexity	How complex is the assignment? Combination of changes on financial, organisational, political, technical and/or personnel level.	
Physical place	Where are the project stakeholders and employees physically located (including PMO)?	*Write down addresses/locations. Special project area(s)?*

APPENDIX B: INTAKE FORM BETWEEN PROJECT MANAGER & PMO EMPLOYEE

Security	Special access requirements?	*Passes, parking, special areas, systems, information. How does it work? Forms? Who to ask?*
Finance	Fixed price/date/result.	*Is the assignment fixated on price and/or time? Which?*
	Costs/benefits. What is the financial bandwidth of costs and benefits (both from client and from steering committee)?	*What is the project budget and how has this been build up and calculated?*
	Rates: Have rates already been issued?	*Which rates have been agreed per product, function, employee?*
	What and how big are the financial risks for the client and for the possible internal client?	
QA	Has the client specified quality expectations?	
	Is there a project quality plan?	
	Are project (or external) audits expected?	*If so, then a proper project file is even more important than usual.*
	Has a quality register been created yet and where is it?	
Steering committee	Has the steering committee been appointed?	*Names, roles.*
<Client>	Who are the stakeholders at the client? Who are the decision makers? (Client, purchasing, project managers)	*Write down names.*
	How many customer departments and/or employees will be affected by the assignment?	*Which?*

APPENDIX B: INTAKE FORM BETWEEN PROJECT MANAGER & PMO EMPLOYEE

<Own organisation>	What is the project's place in the organisation?	
	Who are the stakeholders and decision makers at <Own organisation>? (client, account manager, project managers) Which subsidiary and business units are involved? Is this recorded in an organisation structure?	
	Who is ultimately responsible for the project success?	*Project manager, chairman steering committee, director x, CEO, minister, ...?*
<Third parties>	Are there suppliers? Which? (stakeholders and decision makers)	
	Do any other suppliers need to be involved, appointed for the execution of the assignment?	
Planning	Has the project started already or does it still need to be fully set up?	
	Is there a plan (outlines)? Is it already known to the client, other stakeholders?	
	Are there (sub) project plans and how are these connected to each other?	
	What are the project products?	
Risks	Which risks have already been defined?	*Where can these be found?*
Communi-cation	In which language is being communicated? In which language are the documents drawn up?	
	How formal are the relationships?	
Culture	How is the organisation culture described (open, dynamic, bureaucratic, hostile, suspicious, passive) at the various parties?	

APPENDIX B: INTAKE FORM BETWEEN PROJECT MANAGER & PMO EMPLOYEE

2. PMO assignment (general)

Finance	PMO budget and margin: Does the proposition/contract take into account PMO deployment? If so, how many? Can the margin on the project/contract be increased by decreasing deployment of the project manager and increasing PMO deployment?	*Based on this you can claim a number of extra PMO employees if required. Depending on complexity, size project etc., they can be moved around.*
PMO position	Where does PMO come under? Programme manager, steering committee, project manager, permanent PMO?	
	Is there an existing PMO initiative within the organisation to which you may or need to connect?	
Project management	Is in the contract explicitly being asked for project or programme management by a project manager including a PMO?	*When PMO is included in the contract, the added value will be recognised.*
	Is there commitment for the PMO (role) in all organisational levels?	
Project manager versus PMO	What do you expect from the PMO (and of me)?	*First open question, subsequently you can continue asking.*
	Can you tell me something about yourself?	*Ask the project manager.*
	What do I expect from you?	*Tell your expectations to the project manager.*
	How do you want the communication between us?	*For example, weekly.*

3. Tooling

Project methodology	Which project methodology is being used?	
Mandatory tools/ templates	Are there any requirements to the usage of hardware or software related tools?	
	Are there mandatory templates to use?	*For example for reports, minutes?*

APPENDIX B: INTAKE FORM BETWEEN PROJECT MANAGER & PMO EMPLOYEE

Finance & Time requirements	Time writing and reports.	Which tool? Which process should be followed?
Share documents	SharePoint Server, Directory or other tooling?	
Project planning tool	MS-Project, MS-Excel or other application?	
Internal project communication	How is being communicated? E-mail, monthly updates, team site, daily/weekly project soapbox.	Do they expect a PMO role there?
Facilities	Is internet required to communicate, to share documents etc.? Is it everywhere available, especially at the client? Is internet usage freely accessible?	Or should this be requested?
	Can/may own laptops be used on the client's network?	
	Is/are there (colour) printers available?	Queue names, toners, paper?
	Meeting rooms and work spaces freely available?	How many, where, how to book?
	Have project employees got their own toolkit available (laptops with required software etc.)?	Or should PMO organise this?

4. Set up and align PMO task package

Project set-up & closure	Is there clarity yet on how many project employees are being deployed? Is there a phone directory yet with names of project employees and people involved?	If not, it should be created by PMO QUICKLY. And also maintained.
	Which process do we agree on for on and offboarding of project employees?	How will PMO be timely informed?
	Should PMO organise and manage a steering committee/client governance workshop?	
	Should PMO organise and manage a project kick-off?	

APPENDIX B: INTAKE FORM BETWEEN PROJECT MANAGER & PMO EMPLOYEE

Stakeholder management	Should PMO create a stakeholder register and/or analysis?	
	Should PMO create an activity calendar (including meeting schedule)?	
	Should PMO make presentations for certain stakeholder groups?	*For example on progress project*
	Should PMO facilitate (organise and manage) stakeholder workshops?	*Which?*
Communication	Will there be/is there a communication plan? Who are involved in it, executers?	*Should PMO set up communication plan?*
	Any ideas yet on how to tackle the communication? Communication strategy?	*Should PMO work these out?*
	Should there be a site with information about the project?	*How and where? Should PMO do that?*
	Should there be a Q&A or FAQ maintained? For the project internally? For potential users of the project result?	*How and where? Should PMO do that?*
	Should newsletters be written (internal, external,...)?	*How, where and about what? Should PMO do that?*
Planning	Who makes the project plan? Who keeps the schedule updated? Are there sub schedules that need to be merged?	*Project manager or PMO?*
	Should the schedule be imported in a tool?	*Which?*
	Who maintains PBS? Where is the PBS (Product Breakdown Structure)?	
	Are work packages described?	*By whom, how, where, process?*
	Who creates the dependencies overview?	
	Who monitors achieving of milestones?	
	Should PMO conduct a critical path analysis?	

APPENDIX B: INTAKE FORM BETWEEN PROJECT MANAGER & PMO EMPLOYEE

Resource management	Should PMO do resource management? And maintain resource register?	*How? Which departments involved? Process? Forms?*
	Do contracts or work assignments need to be drafted up?	*Are suppliers already known, make agreements, procedures, forms?*
	Should PMO support employees in terms of organising work area, accounts, access building(s)?	*On and offboarding*
	Does PMO need to do capacity planning or will the project manager do this himself?	
	Should invoices received be compared with scheduled capacity?	
Report	Should the PMO write reports or will the project manager do that himself?	*Which? Frequency? When (what day/time)? Who supplies information (or where to retrieve it)? Who monitors?*
	Has it become clear already which reports should be delivered to whom, when?	*Where should it go to (client/internal)?*
Risk management	Who maintains the risk register? Ensures that new risks are being added? Monitors follow up of risk responses? Where do we place these?	*Who maintains these, how (which process) and where? Should PMO set up the process?*
	Should PMO organise and manage a risk management workshop?	
Issue management	Who maintains issue register and monitors follow up? Where do we place these?	*Who maintains these, how (which process) and where? Should PMO set up this process?*
	Is exception management also being done?	*Who maintains these, how (which process) and where?*
Change control	Change management / Request For Change (RFC) management (record, maintain, prioritise, expand etc.). Also the decisions on changes.	*Who maintains these, how (which process) and where?*
	Should PMO do QA on the changes, modifications and the process?	

APPENDIX B: INTAKE FORM BETWEEN PROJECT MANAGER & PMO EMPLOYEE

Information and configuration management	Is there a formal configuration management method in use? Documents structure?	*How is this being communicated (imposed) to the project employees?*
	Are/will project products uniquely identified?	*According to which agreements?*
	Are/will relationships between project products identified?	
	Which project products will be formally signed?	
	Which version characteristics do products get?	*How is this being communicated (imposed) to the project employees?*
	Are/will all old versions saved?	*How and where?*
	Should PMO archive documents?	*Both digitally and physically? Where?*
Finance	Should budgeting be done by PMO or is it covered in the organisation with an financial department?	*Request budget sheet.*
	Should PMO monitor the budget utilisation (in terms of obligations, invoices and hours)?	*According to which process? Methodologies?*
	Should PMO take on a monitoring, controlling, driving role in terms of invoicing (on contract delivery, RFCs)?	*According to which process?*
	Who sets up the financial progress report & dashboard?	*PMO? According to which periodic?*
	How will the financial impact of a change be processed and by whom?	*PMO?*
Quality management	Should the PMO review documents, for example: • Manuals • PIDs (Project Initiation Document) • Communication plans • FAQ etc.	*Try to estimate the size with regards to the planning of your time or possibly extra PMO resources.* *Check products based on the product descriptions.*
	Should PMO do project assurance? Ensure that the organisation does not slip off to lower quality levels?	

APPENDIX B: INTAKE FORM BETWEEN PROJECT MANAGER & PMO EMPLOYEE

		Which process is being used with respect to approval of products?	*Should PMO set up this process?*
		Who maintains the quality register?	*Project manager or PMO?*
		Is a project monitoring checklist being used? Should PMO check/monitor this?	
Knowledge management		Is the PMO also a focal point for all project related questions (sort of helpdesk)? Is there a functional PMO user account/mailbox?	*If not, organise as soon as possible and ensure that a minimum of 3 people actively monitor and follow these up daily.*
		Where can lessons learned be retrieved for the start of the project?	*What do we do with it in terms of process?*
		Where are lessons learned being documented/saved during the project?	*Who does the management and securing of the lessons learned?*
		Who creates a document for potential new project employees (the project, the environment, facts etc.)?	*Objective is shortened training time new project employees.*
		Should a lessons learned session being organised and managed?	*By PMO?*
		Who sets up project evaluation?	*Project manager or PMO?*
Benefit management		Who quantifies the benefits?	
		Where and by whom are measures recorded for achieving the benefits?	*Project manager or PMO?*
		Who monitors the measures? The controlling of the degree of achieving the established benefits?	*Project manager or PMO?*
		Who sets up a benefit realisation plan?	

APPENDIX B: INTAKE FORM BETWEEN PROJECT MANAGER & PMO EMPLOYEE

Further project management support	Central action list.	*Who maintains these, how (which process) and where?*
	Should meetings be organised (meetings, project kick-off, lessons learned)?	*Which secretary can do this for you? Or should someone additionally be hired for this?*
	Should calendars be kept, organised?	*Which secretary can do this for you? Or should someone additionally be hired for this?*
	How important is it that decisions are being recorded?	*Who maintains these, how (which process) and where?*
	How should correspondence, agreements, e-mails, minutes, invoices etc. be documented (archive function for possible future audits, claims, questions etc.)?	

Additionally	Are there additional matters expected of a PMO?	

The project manager might not be able to answer some questions. To get these, you should go and look elsewhere in the organisation.

If you have been deployed as PMO employee in your "own" organisation, a number of matters from this questionnaire will probably already be known to you.

APPENDIX C: TEMPLATE POP-UP PMO OBJECTIVES AND AGREEMENTS

Consider this template as a sort of charter or work package and submit it to the project manager for approval.

Objective of the pop-up PMO	What the temporary PMO stands for in one sentence.
Available budget	
Duration	For setting up PMO and how long the PMO has to stay operational.
To what extent should the PMO provide support, monitor and be directive?	
Which processes and services will this PMO deliver during the project?	Possibly also indicate phasing.
PMO organisation and staffing	Type or level PMO employee (possibly per PMO or project phase).
PMO stakeholders	With which (staff) departments will the PMO work together?
PMO critical success factors	Which conditions need to be met for the PMO to achieve its objective?
Who checks the quality of the PMO and based on what criteria?	
<To complete on one's own with matters that are important to clarify and align>	

APPENDIX D: POP-UP PMO SETUP CHECKLIST

This checklist is a tool. Certain matters might not apply or you might miss something.

Facility services:

Tasks	Notes	Date completed
Organise access	Passes, parking spaces, special areas, systems.	
Organise project area		
Organise internet access (possibly via UMTS hub)	If you are on location without a wired internet connection, you can get a wireless router (with print server port). This cannot be organised at every client (government).	
Set up joint platform for information and document exchange	Access to intranet or organise project management tool.	
Organise USB stick	As a backup for sharing documents and/or drivers.	
PMO e-mail address/organise mailbox	Functional mailbox for a project questions and communication.	
Printer	Organise project printer(s) and ascertain how to connect. USB stick with printer driver and instruction on connecting to printer.	
Request (or create) contact list of key people	Who are the key stakeholders (function, role in project, e-mail address, telephone number, location)?	
Meet secretary(ies) of key people	As far as you have not done that already after the intake. And also with other PMO related roles (control, purchasing, HR, reproduction, etc.).	
Organise meeting rooms	Ascertain how you can book them.	
Organise conference card for conference calls	Chairman/participant code.	

APPENDIX D: POP-UP PMO SETUP CHECKLIST

Video conferencing	Ascertain how to book and where.	
Determine templates/company style for the project	To be requested at the permanent PMO, use customer templates or create yourself.	
Organise office supplies	Pens, notepads, staplers and staples, tape etc. For workshops: brown paper, post-its, flip chart, markers, tape.	
Find out opening times offices	(In connection with closing times office.) How can you organise overtime? What are canteen and reproduction times?	
Organise number of applications for yourself	- MS Project - Acrobat Professional - MS Visio - etc. Provided you need these, are being used within the (client) organisation and the costs have been agreed upon.	

PMO matters (in consultation with project manager):

Tasks	Notes	Date completed
Organise internal kick-off meeting	Meet and align responsibilities with and between project managers/team leaders.	
Organise kick-off/workshop meeting with the client	If this has not taken place yet.	
Organise team building event	Internally or with the client, if budget permits.	
Set up shared calendar	Probably organise a separate meeting.	
Set up and discuss project rules	Which rules do we apply by as project team?	
Determine project governance	Who reports to whom and when?	
Request or create organogram(s)	Internal, client, project (teams).	

APPENDIX D: POP-UP PMO SETUP CHECKLIST

What does PMO do?	What does PMO do and when? Who does what with more than 1 PMO employee?	
Set up and maintain project file/folder	Create and send instructions to team.	
Set up "project wall"	Physically or at project site. Visualise progress project, structures, workflows etc. Of course this can also be done in a special project management tool.	
Suppliers and partner involvement	Which partners are involved? Which meetings take place periodically? How do we deal with them? Where are the contracts? Which delivery agreements have been made?	
Internal project communication	Newsletters, project site, periodic project staff meeting. Communication calendar.	
Collect information on project and client	Contract, internet/intranet, newspaper, annual report. And stay up to date. Which adjacent projects are there?	

Set up processes and services:

Tasks	Notes	Date completed
Issue register	Where, who, how?	
Action list(s)	Where, who, how?	
Risk register	Where, who, how?	
Deviations or findings	Where, who, how?	
Change management	Where, who, how?	
Risk management	Where, who, how?	
Schedules	Which ones will be created and who maintains them?	

APPENDIX D: POP-UP PMO SETUP CHECKLIST

PBS	Containing all products that the project will deliver. Ensure that PMO always receives a copy at product deliveries, in order to record the status of products.	
Acceptance and completions	Record acceptance criteria. Discuss with client in which form and through which medium documents will be delivered.	

Finance:

Tasks	Notes	Date completed
Meet with controller	Align process. Clarify who does what PMO versus controller.	
Ascertain baseline	Offer calculation.	
Rates	With which (hourly) rates are being calculated?	
Invoice agreements	Who does that? When? What are the triggers?	
A description of project management processes	Whereby the connection of the project with the line organisation should be clear.	
Utilisation of project budget	Who maintains this? How to register direct and indirect project costs? A basic calculation model that is tailored per project, in which used hours/euros are compared with the prognosis.	
Hour prognosis and timesheets/hour approval	Where, who, how?	
Project budget report	Weekly? Per month?	
Change management	Include in budget utilisation registration.	
Project business case and benefit tracking	Execute a baseline measurement (measuring the effect). Set up KPIs to monitor the impact.	

APPENDIX D: POP-UP PMO SETUP CHECKLIST

Resource management:

Tasks	Notes	Date completed
Phone list of all project stakeholders and their role	Very useful also for internal and external e-mailings. Internally at PMO concerning hiring contract information (till when, rate agreement).	
Holiday schedule	Record and make agreements on maintaining.	
Onboarding project employees	Create an A4 (or 2) explaining what the project entails and what the project, location and client rules are. This is handed out to every new project employee (during project take-in). Organisation chart. Access (physically and systems).	
Offboarding project employees	Cancel access. File transfer. Evaluation. Remove from overviews.	
Inventory of training needs	Of project employees.	
Set up knowledge transfer	Training inventory, communication, client involvement in project etc.	

APPENDIX E: POP-UP PMO CLOSURE CHECKLIST

Tasks	Notes	Date completed
Communication end assignment - stakeholders - customers - suppliers - contacts in organisation	• Official announcement in preparation of discharge by project manager. • Final handover by PMO. • Terminate collaboration in project or programme context. • Suspend project organisation.	
Lessons learned information	Provide information to the project manager when compiling the project or programme evaluation.	
End Project/Programme Report information	Provide information and support to the project manager when drawing the final report.	
Finish file	Where will it be archived? Place everything on CD-ROM? Suspend sites/shares etc. Delete all non-relevant and unofficial data from the various systems, like e-mails, meeting requests, memos etc. Has everything been archived and handed over?	
Phase out workplace	Leave behind the area where the project team and PMO have resided "clean".	
Finance	Has everything been invoiced? Outstanding points transferred to controller? Ensure that costs/hours cannot be booked on the project anymore, or transfer these cost units to the BAU. Create overview of the outstanding commitments.	
Review and evaluation	Execute team review, lessons learned session.	
Discharge letter	PMO requests for discharge at the project manager and the steering committee on the work carried out by him/her during the assignment period.	

APPENDIX E: POP-UP PMO CLOSURE CHECKLIST

Make appointment Post Project/Program Review	Schedule an appointment with the client and the project manager to perform an evaluation after 1 to 2 months to be able to determine whether the objectives are actually measurably being achieved.	
Prepare future reviews	Potentially make arrangements with the project manager and the client on review assignments or follow up assignments after 4 to 6 months.	
Plan final project/programme meeting	Organise a fitting closure for all project/programme employees, depending on the financial budget. Successes should be celebrated.	
Say goodbye	E-mail to project team + client team. Thank client and secretary(ies).	

APPENDIX E: POP-UP PMO CLOSURE CHECKLIST

What will be transferred to the Business As Usual (BAU) or permanent PMO and what to the management organisation?

Part that the pop-up PMO transfers to:	BAU organisation	Management organisation
All configuration changes as they have been maintained in the CMDB (Configuration Management Database).		√
Request change (handled and outstanding changes). Within PRINCE2 the follow-on-action-recommendations is being filled in and discussed in the final steering committee meeting. This also includes the transfer to the BAU.	√	
Issue or findings register (handled and outstanding issues or findings).		√
Archive: - Official documentation - Reports - Contracts - Invoices - Client details - Details of employees	- √ - √ - √ - √ - √ - √	- √ - √
Schedule (in time and money).	√	
Management information (physically and digitally).	√	
Deliverables: - User manual - Technical documentation - Installation manuals		- √ - √ - √
Resource information: - Details of employees - Presence overviews - Timesheets	- √ - √	- √
Quality documentation.	√	√
Risk register.	√	√
Authorisations issued for buildings and systems.		√

SOURCES

A4 Project management. Een overzicht van de methode, René Hombergen, Van Haren Publishing, May 2009, 3rd edition ("A4 Project management. An overview of the method" Only available in Dutch)

A guide to the project management body of knowledge (PMBOK Guide), Project Management Institute, 2009, 4th edition

Accelerating Your Project Using Facilitated Work Sessions, Jan Means & Tammy Adams, PMI, conference paper, 2005

Business driven PMO setup, Practical insights, techniques and case examples for ensuring success, Mark Price Perry, J. Ross publishing, 2009

"Captainitis" by Shari Frisinger, on YouTube

Competence profiles, Certification levels and Functions in the Project Management and Project Support Field – Based on ICB version 3, Van Haren Publishing, 2nd edition, 2011

The Power of Scrum, Jeffrey V Sutherland, Rini van Solingen, Eelco Rustenberg, CreateSpace Independent Publishing Platform, 2012

Directing a Change, A guide to Governance of Project Management, Association for Project Management (APM), 2005

Een praktische PMO, De route naar succesvol projectmanagement, Henny Portman, Dialoog, 2011, 1st edition ("A practical PMO, The route to successful project management" Only available in Dutch)

Empowering Employees Through Delegation, Robert Nelson, Irwin Professional Publishing, 1993

Gamestorming: A Playbook for Innovators, Rulebreakers, and Changemakers, Dave Gray, Sunni Brown and James Macanufo, O'Reilly Media, 2010

IJsverkopen aan Eskimo's, Pascelle van Goethem, Business Contact, February 2012 ("Selling ice cream to the Eskimos" Only available in Dutch)

Hartelijk Gefaciliteerd, succesvol veranderen met de workshopaanpak, Jeroen Blijsie and Annet Noordik, Kluwer, 2008 ("Happy Facilitated, changing successfully with the workshop approach" Only available in Dutch)

Het groot verbeterboek, Neil Webers, Lucas van Engelen and Thom Luijben, Academic Service, 2012 ("The great improvement book" Only available in Dutch)

Het Project Management Office – PMO, Jan Willem Donselaar & Remco te Winkel, Van Haren Publishing, 2009 (Only available in Dutch)

IPMA-PMO "Eerste opzet Profielen PjMO, PgMO en PfMO 0.1" Can be downloaded via http://www.pmwiki.nl/group/pmo-midden ("First draft Profiles PjMO, PgMO and PfMO 0.1" Only available in Dutch)

IPMA Projectie Magazine edition 02-2010, Kennismanagement in projecten, Nicoline Mulder and Steven de Groot ("Knowledge management in projects" Only available in Dutch)

SOURCES

IPMA Projectie Magazine edition 03-2010, Competente projectondersteuning, Henny Portman and Jan Willem Donselaar ("Competent project support" Only available in Dutch)

IPMA Projectie Magazine edition 05-2011, Projectbeheersing op 3 factoren, Rob Matser, PQR ("Project management on 3 factors" Only available in Dutch)

Kennismanagement in projecten, Steven de Groot, Dilyana Simons, Eburon, 2011 ("Knowledge management in projects" Only available in Dutch)

Leading successful PMOs, How to build the best project management office for your business, Peter Taylor, Gower Publishing Limited, 2011

Management of Portfolios MoP, OGC, 2011

PM Network, article Don't leave home without it, Matt Alderton, November 2012

Project Driven Creation, Jo Bos, Ernst Harting & Marlet Hasselink. Phaos, 2014, 1st edition

Project Management Survey Report, KPMG, July 2013

Projectmanagement voor opdrachtgevers - De vier principes van succesvol opdrachtgeverschap, Michiel van der Molen, Van Haren Publishing, 2013 ("Project management for project executives - The four principles of successful project governance" Only available in Dutch)

Portfolio, Programme and Project Management Maturity Model – P3M3, Rod Sowden, Axelos, 2013

Portfolio, Programme and Project Offices (P3O), Axelos, second edition 2013

PRINCE2 2009 Glossary of Terms, APM Group, 29 September 2009

Prince2 minus kwaliteit is PINO, Wiebe Zijlstra, ZBC kennisbank, 17 February 2011, http://zbc.nu/ ("Prince2 minus quality is PINO", not available anymore)

Product-Based Planning, Adri Platjes in SCHIP&WERF de ZEE, April 2007 (Only available in Dutch)

Project Governance, Ralf Müller, Gower Publishing, 2009

Project Governance: A Practical Guide to Effective Project Decision Making, Ross Garland and Kogan Page, Philadelphia, 2009

Project Management Office implementeren op basis van P3O®, Jan Willem Donselaar & Tjalling Klaucke, Van Haren Publishing, 2010 ("Implementing project management office based on P3O®" Only available in Dutch)

Projectmanagement na vandaag, John Hermarij and Michiel Louweret, Dialoog, 2012 ("Project management after today" Only available in Dutch)

Quality Assurance in projecten. Wiebe Zijlstra, ZBC kennisbank, 23 February 2011, http://zbc.nu ("Quality Assurance in projects" Only available in Dutch)

Regel jij het draagvlak?, Monica Wigman, De Communicatiepraktijk, 2011, 1st edition ("Will you organise the baseline?" Only available in Dutch)

Researching the Value of Project Management, PMI, Mullaly and Thomas, 2009

Risicomanagement op basis van M_O_R® en NEN/ISO 31000, Douwe Brolsma and Mark Kouwenhoven, Van Haren Publishing, 2012 ("Risk management based on M_O_R® and NEN/ISO 31 000" Only available in Dutch)

Second order of project management, Michael Cavanagh, Ashgate Publishing, 2011

SOURCES

Start With Why: How Great Leaders Inspire Everyone to Take Action, Simon Sinek, Portfolio Trade, 2011

http://www.deloitte.com/assets/Dcom-Netherlands/Local%20Assets/Documents/NL/Diensten/Consulting/nl_nl_Consulting_CIO_Magazine_Baat_bij_effectief_benefits_management_okt09.pdf (Only available in Dutch)

Uw hofnar "Spreek van de week" SMS service of Marco Raad and Hans Gestman (Your court jester "Weekly saying" Only available in Dutch)

Visual meetings, David Sibbet

Waarom doen we dit eigenlijk? De businesscase als succesfactor voor projecten, Michiel van der Molen, Van Duuren Management, 2010 ("Why do we actually do this? – The business case as success factor for projects" Only available in Dutch)

Wegwijzer voor methoden bij projectmanagement, Ariane Moussault, Edwin Baardman, Fritjof Brave, Van Haren Publishing, 2011, 2nd edition ("Project management methodologies roadmap" Only available in Dutch)

ACKNOWLEDGEMENTS

A lot of help has been given to me when writing, publishing and marketing this book. I would therefore like to give a big thanks to everyone who has directly or indirectly helped me with this.

In particular:
- Mark Kouwenhoven of nThen!, who gave me the necessary positive boost to actually write this book. We have been thinking about metaphors of which "The wedding planner for projects" was also an option at the time.
- Bart Verbrugge of Van Haren Publishing, for all his advice on the structure and content of the book. Without him there would not have been a chapter on competences and personal goals.
- Loekie Paardekooper of KPN Consulting, for her contribution on resource management.
- Annet Noordik of Hartelijk Gefaciliteerd, for making the workshop flow chart available, her input and review of the chapter "Along with everyone".
- Carleen Sikkema for all her editorial checking and suggestions.
- Hennes and Mauritz for providing the photo of the pop-up shop container on the beach of Scheveningen.
- André Grimbergen of printing company Quantus, for his advice and help.
- Ronald van Klooster and Rob Steenbrink of Maxlead, for their advice and design of the (online) marketing.
- My home front for all the hours in which I spent too much time behind the computer and was "no fun" to them.

And thanks to all the reviewers:
Carleen Sikkema (Capgemini)
Foekje Schreuder (ABN AMRO)
Frank Oeben (Ordina)
Henny Portman (ING Insurance & Investment)
Judith Engelberts (Win Project Support)
Mark Kouwenhoven (nThen!)
Ron Vinken (KPN)
Wijnand Lens (Dolgoz)

INDEX

Acceptance 113, 114, 122
   acceptance criteria 109, 114, 125, 128, 150, 200
   acceptance test 110, 139
   acceptance agreement 110
   acceptance declaration 121
   acceptors 109, 114, 122
accountant 103
acronyms 81, 111, 141, 144
activity calendar 190
agenda management 137
   agenda(s) 17, 47, 141, 142
agile 3, 43, 52, **57-59**, 62-63, 105, 132
APMG 156, 159
Archive/ing 46, 117, 118, 120, 121, 123, 140, 193, 202
ASL 126
Axelos i, 1, 2, 4, 9, 10, 22, 86
audit(s) 40, 85, 110, 118, 120, **123, 181,** 187, 195
   audit requirements 109
   audit proof 140

Backlog (product-) 57, 63, 97, **183**
balanced scorecard 79, **181**
baseline 40, 54, **59-61**, 73, 97, 120, 128, 200
BAU (Business As Usual) 21, 24, 26, 52, **180**, 204
benefits management **73-77**
   benefit(s) 1, 2, 39, 47, 135, 148, 150, **181**, 185, 187, 194
billing 103, 104, 106
BISL 126
budget 27, 29, 31, 34- 36, 49, 58, 60-62, 65-68, 76, 82, 88, 97, 99, **103-107**, 150, 151, 154, **181**, 187, 189, 193, 196, 198, 200, 203
business case 14, 54, **73-76**, 103-104, 112, 148, **181**, 186, 200
business change manager 40, 73, 126
business model canvas 74, 146

Capabilities 16, 29
capacity (PMO-) 33, 35-36, 39, 43
capacity (project-) 65, 67, 70, 115, 192
captainitis 173-174
CAB (Change Advisory Board) 40, 97, 99, 125, 128

INDEX

change management 1, 33, 40, 61, 74, **97-101**, 160, 192, 199, 200
classify / classification 53, 118
client 17, 18, 24, 47, 54, 58, 59, 61-63, 67, 73, 76, 79-82, 85, 91, 97, 99-101, 105, 110, 112, 117, 123, 125-127, 131, 137, 148-152, 168, 185, 186-188, 190, 197-201, 203, 204
confidentiality 123
     - form 69
closure (project) 38, **45-49**, 73, 125-126
   closure checklist 201
communication 6, 7, 25, 30-31, 36, 38, 47, **50-55**, 63, 81, 86, 101, 109, 128, 137, 143, 148, 149, 152, 153, 155, 167, 189, 191, 193, 197, 199, 201, 202
   communication officer or manager 1, 160
   communication (-visual) 146
competences 2, 19, 33, 41, 63, 67, 132, **156-163**, 171
compliance 13, 109, **182**
configuration management 4, 6, 40, 57, 100, **117-123**, 153, 193, 204
conspiracy of optimism 89
contacts (list) 28, 31, 45, 53, 139, 197, 202
contract(s) 17, 29, 46, 63, 65, 68-70, 85, 97, 101, 117, 119-121, 123, 126, 127, 149, 150, 154, 186, 189, 192, 193, 199, 201, 204
controller 7, 17, 19, 21, 27, 35, 79, 103, 105, 117, 158, 160, 200, 202
corporate board 15, 131
costs 6, 46, 58, 60, 61, 63, 65, 68, 76, 81, 86, 98-100, **103-107**, 108, 127, 133, 149, 175, 176, 187, 198, 200, 202
critical chain planning 58
critical path 57, 191

Dashboard 36, 103, 193
decision (making) 16, 74, 149
decision register 120, 138, **141**, 150
delegate 33, 36, 43, 112, 149, 174, **175-176**
department(s) 27, 65, 85, 99, 122, 187, 192, 196
    - commercial, purchasing or procurement 40, 65
    - communication 51, 52
    - financial 103, 193
    - HR 65, 67
    - ICT (service) 45, 51
    - PMO 2, 8, 19
dependency/ies 39, 57, 58, 60, 85, 150
   - overview 191
devil's triangle 61, 62

INDEX

directory (-structure) 120, 190
discharge 48, 125, 126, 202
    - Form 46
Document(s) / -ation 23, 46, 48, 59, 73, 85, 86, 97, 110, 111, 114, **117-123**, 125, 126, 131, 137, 141, 152, 188, 190, 193-195, 197, 200, 204

Elevator pitch 169
e-mail 45, 48, 55, 69, 70, 117, 120, 121, 168, 190, 195, 197, 201, 202, 203
EMV (Expected Monetary Value) 88
end user(s) 17, 114, 125, 128, 131, 132, 185
escalation(s) 17, 29, 34, 36, 39, 91, 104, 113, 114, 122, 150
EVA (Earned Value Analysis) 60, 104, 105
evaluate /-tion(s) 55, 66, 71, 86, 89, 110, 132, 134, 135, 201
    - project 49, 132, 194, 202, 203
exception management 192
    exception(s) 82, 150, **182**

Facilitating sessions / workshop 144, 151, 154, 160
    facilitator 144, 151
facility /-ies 1, 3, 10, 13, 26, 27, 38, 40, 45, 46, 65, 125, 131, 137, 138, 139, 152, 190, 197
finance(s) 6, 33, 40, 49, 89, **103-107**, 120, 153, 187, 189, 190, 193, 200, 202
financial 17, 29, 40, 46, 48-49, 65, 76, 79, 86, 97, 99, 118-119, 122-123, 128, 154, 155, 186-187, 193, 203
findings 199, 204
    findings register 95
fixed price / costs 13, 59, 67, 82, 101, 105, 187
force field analysis 47, 52

Governance 6, **13-18**, 21, 23, 24, 29, 45, 46, 123, 172, **182**, 190, 198
    governance (-corporate) 14, 15, 21

Hire register 70
holiday (schedule) 29, 30-31, 66-67, 70, 201
hours / hourly 26-27, 34, 47, 65, 67-68, 70, 104-105, 107, 132, 140, 153-154, 193, 200, 202

Information (management) 13, 21, 23, 25, 27, 30, 40, 57, **117-123,** 128, 146, 148, 153, 160, 191-193, 197, 204
ishikawa diagram 86
ISO 110

INDEX

issue management 39, **91-95**, 120, 153, 192
issue register (log) 91, 93, **95**, 98, 192, 199
intake (conversation between project manager and PMO employee) 17, 27, 154
    intake form between project manager and PMO employee **186-195**
invoice(s) 48, 49, 65, 103, 105, 106, 192, 193, 195, 200, 202
IPMA 2, 9, 11, 12, 38-41, 82, 156-159, 160, 161, 163
iteration(s) 28, 31, 57, 59, 60, **62-63**, 105, 118, 132, **182**
ITIL 2, 126

Kick-off 13, 14, 31, 45-47, 57, 76, 137, 143, 147, **148-150**, **183**, 190, 195, 198
knowledge 29, 30, 33, 59, 67, 68, 82, 113, 117, 128, 160, 163, 164, 165168, 169, 170, 175, 201
    knowledge center 2, 23, 143, **181**
    knowledge management 41, 48, 63, **131-135**, 153, **183**, 194
KPI (Key Performance Indicator) 36, 82, **182**

Learning matrix 132
legal 86, 89, 118, 119, 122, 140
lessons learned 41, 45, 46, 48, 49, 59, **131-135**, 143, **183**, 194, 195, 202
    lessons learned register 131, **135**
library 117, 132
line organization 8, 24, 38, 48, 134, 200
locations 6, 45, 65, 66, 186
logbook 55, 109, 110, 131

(e-)Mail 45, 48, 55, 69, 70, 93, 117, 120, 121, 168, 190, 195, 201-203
    mailbox 30, 45, 47, 55, 69, 194, 197
mandate(d) 38, 45, 149, 150, 151, 186
maturity 16, 21, 22, 67, 133, 155, 162
meeting(s) 17, 29, 35-36, 40, 46-47, 51, 53, 55, 58, 69, 93-94, 106, 110, 121-122, 134, 137, 139-142-143-146, 151-152, 154-155, 169, 182-183, 190, 191, 195, 197-199, 202-204
methodologie(s) 2-4, 21, 43, 62, 85, 193
minutes (meeting-) 61, 122, 137, 138, **140-142**, 154, 189, 195
mitigate 87, 149
milestones 17, 55, 57, 60, 76, 82, 103, 117-119, 150, **183**, 186, 191
money 6, 60-61, 74, 81, 102, 108, 128, 150, 179, 181, 183, 186, 204
monitor(ing) 2, 15, 17, 21, 23, 39-40, 52, 57-59, 66, 73-74, 79-80, 82, 85-86, 88, 91-93, 95, 97, 103, 109, 112, 114-115, 134, 140, 144, 146, 149, 152, 160, 172, 183, 191-194, 196, 200
MSP (Managing Succesful Programmes) 2-4, 9, 43, 48, 74

INDEX

multiproject 2

Naming (conventions) 57, 60, 117, 119, **122**
newsletter 32, 52, 55, 69, 121, 191, 199
newspaper 51, 199
NPV (Net Present Value) technique 104

Objective(s) 5, 8-13, 25, 26, 38-41, 140-142, 144, 165, 184, 194, 196
   - project / programme 1, 7, 14-18, 53-55, 74, 77, 87, 99, 131, 134, 182, 185, 186, 203
   - strategic 2, 76, 183
occupancy 29
offboarding 46, **69**, 190, 192, 201
offer (calculation) 107, 200
office supplies 137, 198
onboarding 46, **69**, 190, 192, 201
owner 73, 86, 182, 185
   ownership 143, 148, 149
   - issue 93-94, 151
   - product 51, 63, 105
   - risk 86-88

P3O i, 1, 2, 4, 9-11, 18, 27, 38-42, 117, 155, 156, 158, 159
PBS Product Breakdown Down 47, 58-61, 63, 67, 70, 97, 111. 114-115, 121-122, 125, 149, **183**, 191, 200
permanent PMO 2, 6, 8, 21-23, 33, 37, 38-41, 48, 156, 158, 204
PID (Project Initiation Document) 18, 29, 111, 122, **184**, 193
planning(s) 6, 26, 27, 33-34. 38-39, 42, 47-48, 55, **57-63**, 66, 67, 89. 110, 143, 153, 163, 188, 190-193
portfolio 6, 11, 15, 20, 22, 38, 157, 181, **183**
   - management 1, 9, 80, 157
   - office I, 1, 3, 19, 159
PMBOK 3, 4, 43, 48
PMO functions i, 2, 9, 16, 19, 155, **156-163**
presence overview 204
PRINCE2 2-4, 9, 16, 43, 48, 63, 93, 113, 204
project file (dossier) 38, 45-46, 118, **119-123**, 126, 187, 199
product backlog (see backlog)
product-based planning 58, 149
product descriptions 60, 63, 115, **184**, 193
product owner 51, 63, 105

INDEX

PSU (project Start Up) 46, 47 (see also kick-off)
purchasing 40, 107, 187, 197

Quality (assurance) 24, 29, 33, 34, 36, 40, 61-63, 65, 99, 108, **109-115**, 122, 123, 128, 139, 143, 150, 154, 155, 167, 170, 175, 181, **184**, 186-187, 193, 196, 204
- controller or manager 21, 27, 109, 160, 169
- management 14, 21, 23, 112, 120, 153
- register 97, 110, **115**, 120, 121, 122, 194

Raci / rasci matrix 52, 86
RCA (Root Cause Analysis) 132
report(s) reporting 10, 17, 21, 28, 34, 36, 39, 40, 46, 49, 58, 61, 65, 74, **79-83**, 88, 91, 93-95, 97, 103-106, 109, 113-114, 121, 132, 134, 137-141, 149-150, 153-155, 160, **184**, 189-190, 192, 193, 198, 200, 202, 204
resistance 28, 52, 126, 163
resource(s) 2, 7, 8, 23, 27, 34, 86, 103-104, 121, 131, 149, 154, **184**, 193, 204
- management 17, 39, 46, 58, 63, **65-71**, 97, 153, 160, 192, 201
- resources hire register **70**, 192
retrospective 82, 132, 134
review(s) 17, 23, 33, 39, 57, 71, 73-74, 110, 111, 114, 117, 122, 132, 160, **184**, 193, 202-203
RFC (Request For Change) **182**, 192
roadmap iii, 5-7, 25, 45, 57, 97, 152, **184**
risk(s) 13, 14, 42, 46, 52, 57, 58, 63, 66, 69, 74, 76, 79, 80, 82, 86, 92, 93, 98, 99, 104, 110, 111, 118, 126, 133, 138, 143, 149-150, 182, **184**, 187, 188
- appetite 88, **184**
- capacity 88
- management 33, 39, 63, **85-89**, 93, 121, 153, 169, 192, 199
- manager 19, 29, 158, 160
- register 85, 86, 87, **88**, 89, 97, 192, 199, 204
RISMAN 86

Salami tactics 28
schedule(s) 4, 6, 29, 39, 55, **57-63**, 65-68, 70, 76, 81-83, 97-98, 103, 110, 121, 133, 135, 149, 154, 191, 199, 201, 204
service management 126, 163
scope 6, 47, 61, 63, 76, 77, 97, 99, 105, 128, 143, 150, 181, **184**
scrum 3, 4, 43, 55, 58, 62, 63, 97, 105, 132
secretariat 40, **137-142**, 154
secretary 19, 32, 139-141, 146, 195, 197, 203
security 86, 117, **123**, 187

INDEX

setup checklist 197-201
size (-PMO) 10, 29, 34, **153-155**
soapbox session 55, 137
social media 30, 55, 66, 168, 169
staffing 33, 35, 153, 196
stakeholder management 6, 38, **51-55**, 121, 153
stakeholder(s) 5-7, 11, 15, 42, 45, 46, **51-53**, 57, 59, 63, 65, 73, 79, 82, 85, 86, 91, 97, 100, 103, 109, 113, 117, 125, 131, 137, 149, 155, 182, 186-188, 197, 201
steering committee 14, 17, 18, 58, 70, 79-82, 122, 137, 139-140, 143, 148-150, 182, 183, 185, 187, 202, 204
supplier(s) 3, 17, 40, 46, 58, 65-67, 69, 70, 85, 91, 109, 112, 118, 148, 188, 192, 199, 202
sustainable 5, 15

Tender 27, 65, 85
test(s) 61, 95, 100, 110, 114, 122, 139, 184
   - plan 97, 114
   - testing 112
timesheet(s) 34, 104, 105, 200, 204
tooling 154, 189
tools and tooling 4, 6, 7, 10, 17, 25, 26, 30, 31, 36, 41-43, 46, 52, 57, 58, 62, 63, 66, 67, 70, 74, 79, 81, 83, 85-86, 91, 93, 97-98, 103-104, 109-110, 118, 120, 122, 126, 128, 132, 135, 138, 139, 146, 148, 154, 160, 163, 184, 185, 189-191, 197, 199
transition (management) 34, 35, 40, 48, **125-129**. 153, **185**
   - transfer / red 48, 49, 87, 91, 114, 118, **125-126**, 128, 150, 153, 185, 201, 202, 204
transparency 13, 29, 31, 61, 76, 149
turnover 73, 131, 134

Update(s) \ -ted 31, 32, 46, 57, 59, 61, 69, 73, 82, 85, 91, 103, 105-106, 118-120, 132, 154, 169, 190, 191
utilisation 35, 70, 82, 103, 106, 120, 154, 193, 200

Virtual 2, 69

Wasting 74
waterfall 59
WBS (Work Breakdown Structur) 47, 57, 58, 67, 70, **185**
welcome document 47, 131
workshop 14, 16-18, 39, 46, 51, 58, 59, 74, 85-86, 88, 132, **143-152**, 160, 166, 190-192, 198

Notes:

Notes:

Printed in Great Britain
by Amazon.co.uk, Ltd.,
Marston Gate.